Angus Martin was educated at St Andrew's College, South Africa. He graduated from the University of the Witwatersrand in 1962 with a B.Sc. in Zoology, and in 1968 received his Ph.D. from the University of Melbourne, where he is at present Lecturer in Zoology. Angus Martin's previous book, *Pollution and Conservation in Australia*, was published in 1971, and he frequently contributes articles to scientific journals.

ANGUS MARTIN

The Last Generation

The end of survival?

FONTANA/COLLINS

First published in Fontana 1975
Copyright © Angus Martin 1975

Set in 10 pt Intertype Plantin

Made and printed in Great Britain by
William Collins Sons & Co Ltd Glasgow

Contents

To
my parents
who encouraged me to read books

Antony Trew
who encouraged me to write one

and my wife
who has patiently put up with my
devoting an excessive amount of time
to both occupations

Prologue

'All attempts to answer [the question: What is man?]
before 1859 are worthless and . . . we will be better off
if we ignore them completely.'

Those words were written by George Gaylord Simpson in
1966,[1] and what he meant was this: In 1859 Darwin's *On
the Origin of Species* was published, and for the first time
man had a general explanation of life, of diversity, and of his
own existence. He had a framework, a conceptual scaffold-
ing, in which he could place himself, and from which he
could ask the question, 'What am I?' And at last he knew
where he should be looking for the answers: 'There is no
place', writes R. D. Alexander, 'to seek general explanations
of human nature but in the evolutionary process.'[2]

It could nevertheless be said with some truth that, while
in theory the idea of mankind evolving is all very well, in
practice it didn't help a great deal in formulating a new view
of ourselves. We simply didn't know enough about it: too
many evolutionary concepts were still vague, half-formed;
too few implications for man could be extracted from the
outlines and the shadows. For decades after 1859 one could,
if one so wished, maintain a consistent and defensible position along the lines of: We *can* look at mankind in that way.
But there isn't enough evidence to say that we *must*.

This is not true today. Over the last few years the weight
of evidence bearing on human evolution has become so overwhelming, the hypotheses and explanations have become so
refined, that there is indeed no other sensible context in which

to view man. Man *is* a product of organic evolution; man *has* had a long evolutionary history; man's characteristics cannot be meaningfully examined unless we make this our starting point. To quote once again from Alexander's lucid exposition of the evolutionary viewpoint: 'Whatever we may think or believe about man must be consistent with what we know about evolution and man's history.'

It is perhaps just as important to recognize what this does not mean as what it does mean. It does not, first of all, imply that man is 'just another animal', which is the brickbat most commonly flung at it. But it does imply that, if we take 'animal' to mean 'animate product of organic evolution', then, whatever else man may be, he *is* first and foremost an animal. It does not mean that if we acknowledge man's biological nature and his evolutionary history we shall then be in a position to answer the question: What is man? But it does mean that we cannot even sensibly ask the question if we do not make these acknowledgements. And it does not mean that recognition of these facts will give us a key to our prolonged survival on earth. But then that is something which refusal to recognize the facts will not achieve either. Looking at man in his biological context may not tell us what the solutions are, but it will certainly tell us what they are *not*.

A simple example: Freud and the 'death-instinct'. As a contribution to the aggressive behaviour of some mythical 'man' who transcends nature, a death-instinct is quite in order. But for a man who is a product of natural selection the concept of a death-instinct is clearly rubbish; it is totally at variance with biological principles. The evolutionary biologist may not have a completely satisfactory explanation of human aggression (though I believe he has come closer than anyone else), but he can say: Whatever the cause of human aggression may be, I can absolutely guarantee that it has nothing at all to do with a death-instinct.

I am not going to present any defence of the realities of man's biological nature or man's evolutionary history; these things are by now adequately documented and unquestionably valid. The real point at issue is what we are to make of them, and this is where we still have a long way to go. The evolutionary philosophy of Simpson, Alexander and others should have caused a revolution in our views of ourselves; it hasn't. We still behave as though man's evolutionary history were a mere appendage, a mere layer of icing on the human cake. We continue to try to interpret man without reference to it; we say, in effect: 'Oh yes, we know all about that, but so what? It's only the evolutionary biologists having their fun; *we* (anthropologists, psychologists, medical biologists, historians) shall leave them to it and get on with the job of understanding man.' We still have not grasped that man is not fully comprehensible in any terms but these, which is not of course to say that, at this moment, in them he is fully comprehensible.

One of the factors which makes us unwilling to place ourselves in an evolutionary perspective is undoubtedly the nature of the evolutionary process. We tend to be both goal-oriented and value-oriented in our judgement of concepts; we say, 'Where does it get us? How does it help us? Is it good or bad? What's in it for us?' Those are not the criteria by which evolution proceeds; consequently, evolutionary arguments are frequently not 'satisfying', not 'relevant', not 'useful'. Another simple example: human cannibalism. What should we say of cannibalism: that it's disgusting, that it's bestial, that it's evil and immoral? Natural selection does not say any of those things; all its asks is: Did cannibalism contribute to the fitness (a concept discussed more fully in Chapter 2) of these men in this situation? And if the answer is *yes* then the evolutionary biologist has a sufficient explanation of why cannibalism occurred. No further justification or analysis is required: that is a complete and satisfying answer.

This, of course, is exactly the sort of conclusion which invites the complaint: 'But that doesn't get us anywhere. What are you suggesting we *do* about it?' In the same way evolutionary arguments are often dubbed circular, or non-testable, or even fatalistic. All of which may very well be true, but evolutionary biologists tend not to be too worried about it. '*You're* using the word "fatalistic" (or whatever),' they can justly say – 'not us. All we said was – we think this is why natural selection produced that little piece of behaviour, or structure, or whatever. That's all we were interested in – you can make of it what you like.'

Nevertheless a word or two needs to be said about the thread of fatalism, of predestination, which will be seen to run through this book. The concept of predestination in its everyday sense is a dirty word in the evolutionary context: it implies 'orthogenesis', or straight-line evolution towards some preconceived goal. It implies that the little three- and four-toed horses of the Eocene were 'aiming at', 'striving towards', 'predestined to give rise to', the big one-toed horses of the Pleistocene. This is clearly nonsense; G. G. Simpson's discussion of the question[3] can be consulted for a fuller analysis. But it is also true, as Simpson again points out, that natural selection is a partially deterministic process. Selection can operate only on the material it has at its disposal, and the nature of that material obviously has an important bearing on its future, on what natural selection will make of it. Our two-toed horse may well give rise to a three-toed horse or a one-toed horse; it will hardly give rise to an arboreal fruit-eater, or an aquatic carnivore, or a flying insectivore. The evolutionary future of any lineage is not determined absolutely, but it is determined within limits. To that extent, and in that sense, the evolutionary biologist is a determinist; and if it appears that he is obsessed with fatalism, it is only because he is acknowledging this fact.

Three years ago one of the favourite topics of lunch-hour conversation in the zoology department of the university where I work was the population crisis, spiced with paeans of hatred directed at industries which tipped their cyanide wastes into rivers, and forestry authorities who razed native trees and replaced them by pine plantations. We used to say cynical and sophisticated things like, 'What's the use of sending wheat to Pakistan? Why not just send them a thousand bushels of contraceptive pills?' and 'Why waste money on heart transplants? Why not put it to sterilizing ten million Indians instead?' It came as something of a shock to me to realize that we have now not talked that way for months. What put an end to it, more than anything, was the coda put to his argument by a young biochemist as we got up to wander back to our offices and laboratories. 'We're the last generation who can eat a steak any time we like,' he said, 'and chop down a tree if we feel destructive, and have as many kids as we want. We're privileged; we're the last of our kind. So what the hell: let's make the most of it. Let's *treat* it as a privilege. Why be like the art collector who locks up his priceless paintings in a vault, and never displays them for fear they'll get damaged or stolen? Let's bring 'em out, make the most of 'em: we're the last generation who can.'

Thus the title of this book is not original, and that may also be true of much of its contents. Every biologist at one time or another has the sobering experience of rediscovering what he thought was a great new inspiration in a book which he'd read ten years earlier and forgotten about. Likewise I know of no biologist who, the day after a lively discussion, can say: These and those ideas that we talked about were *mine*. I have acknowledged all my sources where I am aware of them, but there are doubtless numerous unacknowledged statements which I have subconsciously gleaned from the writings and sayings of others. My indebtedness to many evolutionary biologists, and others, will be obvious, but that does not imply that they have read, or that they endorse, what I say. Three warrant special acknowledgement, but no share of the blame: Murray Littlejohn, who led me into the field of evolutionary biology; Richard Alexander, who made me want to stay there; and Garrett Hardin, whose breadth of intellect never ceases to astound me. The point should also be made that the sundry aspersions cast in these pages at people who have tried to get us to look at ourselves in an evolutionary context – Lorenz, Morris, Ardrey, Storr – should not be taken to mean that I disagree with their overall approach; merely with some of their arguments and conclusions. No doubt they have plenty to cast back at me. They are the pioneers, the ice-breakers, the trail-blazers; I, we all, are more indebted to them than to anyone.

NOTES

1 SIMPSON, GEORGE GAYLORD. *Biology and Man* (New York, Harcourt, Brace and World 1969)
2 ALEXANDER, RICHARD D. 'The Search for an Evolutionary Philosophy of Man', *Proceedings of the Royal Society of Victoria*, Vol. 84 (1971), 99–120
3 SIMPSON, GEORGE GAYLORD. *This View of Life* (New York, Harcourt, Brace and World 1964)

1 The Battle is Over

'There's nothing serious in mortality.'

Shakespeare: *Macbeth*

'The battle to feed all of humanity is over.' That sentence, which opens *The Population Bomb*,[1] displays much of the genius of Paul Ehrlich: mastery of the short, pithy phrase that suddenly brings one up short in one's tracks. What do we take that sentence to mean? Obviously, the battle is over because we have won it. We have very rarely acknowledged any other reason for allowing a battle to end. But the next sentence says, 'In the 1970s and 1980s hundreds of millions of people will starve to death . . .' And then one realizes, with something of a shock, that in fact Ehrlich is saying that we've *lost* the battle. That is an inconceivably horrifying thing to say. Hundreds of millions of people will starve to death. He is talking of a tragedy on a scale we have never had to contemplate. How many people died at Hiroshima in August 1945? Eighty thousand. How many died in the great cholera epidemics in England in the middle 1800s? Two hundred thousand. How many were killed by the Black Death in Europe in the fourteenth century. Twenty million. How many died as a direct or indirect result of the Second World War? Sixty million.[2] Even if we use one of those statistician's devices and say: If the coffins of all the people who died as a consequence of the Second World War were piled one on top of another they would form a tower more than 1700 miles high, a fifth of the diameter of the earth, or three hundred times higher than Mount Everest . . . Even then, we cannot conceive of what the deaths of sixty million, or even sixty thousand, people really mean. And now we are being asked to contemplate the deaths – certain, unavoidable deaths – of hundreds of millions of people.

For all that, your reaction when you read those two sentences was probably much the same as mine. An initial chill of horror, and then a mental image of a person starving to death. What was your mental image? Mine was of an Ethiopian woman with her child, probably gleaned from some press account of the current famine. Yours may have been of a Biafran piccaninny suffering from kwashiorkor, or a Vietnamese orphan, or an inmate of Belsen when the Allies arrived. I can be as sure of your image as I am of my own: it wasn't of your mother, or your son, or your secretary, or the family next door. You and I both employed our very considerable talent for making sure that the nasty something stayed far away in the woodshed, and didn't come beating on our own front door.

And then we went on reading *The Population Bomb*. We came to some fascinating scenarios, some biting sarcasm, some gutsy humour, a great many startling statistics, coolly and forcefully employed, some magnificent polemics, some unlikely solutions. And at the end we were left with . . . what? A vague unease, probably; a mild feeling of depression. Things seemed to be in a pretty bad way – smog, DDT, radiation, malnutrition, eutrophication – the list is endless. And . . . 'the battle to feed all of humanity is over'.

Even so, we still don't leap for our typewriters and begin pounding out letters to Parliament, to the Press, to anyone who might listen. Nor do we head for the supermarket to lay in a supply of plastic-wrapped, aluminium-lined, denatured, homogenized and chemically mongrelized food, against the day when the loss of the battle finally catches up with us.

We won't throw away the tin of dieldrin in the garage, or have the exhaust system of the car checked to see how much carbon monoxide it produces. And we certainly won't decide to have only two children, or, perhaps, regret the fact that we already have five.

'How many deaths will it take till they know that too many people have died?' asks Bob Dylan plaintively,[3] and we could ask with him, 'How many people must warn us of our fate before we take them seriously enough to do something about it?' Paul Ehrlich is only one of the many biologists who have been telling us . . . there are also the medical scientists, the economists, the statesmen, the United Nations, the Club of Rome . . . There have been the exquisitely argued and meticulously documented warnings like Garrett Hardin's *Tragedy of the Commons*;[4] there have been the emotion-charged, blood-and-thunder horror stories in the Press. None of it has had very much effect. No country has adopted a 'spaceship economy', the low-production, low-consumption, low-wastage system envisaged by Kenneth Boulding.[5] No national leader has staked his government's life on zero population growth. No medical organization has pledged itself to spend a dollar on birth control research for every cent it spends on death control.

'How many deaths will it take?' Stirring words. 'The battle is over.' Provocative words. But how many words will it take? I am myself guilty of contributing to the flow of verbiage, in a book published in Australia in 1971.[6] In it I said things like: 'the use of DDT has had unexpected and far-reaching consequences', and 'our great hopes of food from the sea are largely wishful thinking', and 'coercion will have to be applied to limit the number of children a couple can have'. The reviewers said 'alarming picture of global genocide', and 'this frightening book', and 'the terrible fate ahead', and 'see the danger and heed the warning'. (They also said 'this is a pleasant-looking book' and 'some of the illustrations are ex-cellent'.) I suppose that for one infinitesimal moment a minute fraction of the population of Australia paused in its tracks. And then it went on and drank more beer, and kicked more footballs, and watched more television, and shot more kangaroos, and had more babies.

When you write a book and no one takes any notice of it you begin to wonder . . . Why? There are three possibilities. Either Ehrlich, Hardin and the rest of them are wrong. That is certainly a possibility, but it is such a remote one that I shall not consider it any further. Or I, and everyone else who has written on the subject, have expressed myself so inef-fectively that the message has simply failed to get across. Or . . .

It is this last 'or' that is the subject of this book. It is the 'or' that can answer the question, How many deaths? and, How many words? It is the 'or' that explains why we can absorb the inevitable deaths of hundreds of millions of people, and barely bat an eyelid.

This is the 'or': *Homo sapiens* is so constituted, has evolved in such a way, has adopted such social systems, and is characterized by such behaviour, that he is incapable of heeding what he is being told. It is a simple practical im-possibility. He is the pig who is being asked to fly, the chim-panzee being asked to paint the Mona Lisa, the Kalahari bushman being asked to programme an IBM computer. It isn't a question of, he could, if only . . . It's a question of an utter and total incapacity.

So the answers to the questions, 'How many deaths?' and 'How many words?' are the same: as many or as few as you like; it will make no difference. And the fact that the battle is over is easy to take in one's stride, because our nervous system is designed to take such things in its stride. And those millions of corpses . . . *we* shall not be among them.

Our genetic programming simply does not allow us to contemplate the possibility.

The battle to feed all of humanity is over. A grim enough message; grimmer ones have rarely been written. And yet Paul Ehrlich does not allow himself to become a victim of his own forebodings. His books always include sections telling us how to avoid the disasters that he foretells in such graphic terms. To consider him merely as a prophet of doom does him less than justice: he is one of the greatest optimists of all time. Knowing what he does, appreciating as he does the totally vitriolic nature of the particular pickle we have got ourselves into, he still believes it worthwhile to devote pages and pages to methods of escape from the pickle jar. He is programmed, like you and me – programmed not to believe his own propaganda. He admits to adhering to a hope, however slim, that the world can be saved; others are convinced that there is no conceivable reason why the world should not be saved, to prosper to the end of time. Their basic philosophy is precisely the same: there is hope yet. So we have something of a paradox. The ecologist talks about contraception, and abortion, and misery, and starvation, and the death of the oceans, and a shattering revolution in our way of life, and believes that the world can be saved. The politician announces increased child endowment and decreased foreign aid, and explains how they will save the world. The man next door recites a little chant about how malaria was defeated, and how the moon was invaded, and how Science will come up with 'something' to save the world. All start from different premises; all come to the same conclusion. Why such unanimity? Because there is no alternative: the human computer simply lacks the capacity to come out with any other answer.

And yet, in recent years, running in parallel with this optimism, this naïve faith, has been a distinct 'Where have we gone wrong?' element in our view of ourselves. The point needs to be made that we have *not* gone wrong, that we have achieved everything we set out to achieve. The human experiment has indeed been a remarkable one, and not the least remarkable thing about it has been its success. Raymond Dart[7] made a perceptive statement in the course of his *Nature* article (7 February 1925) on the human ancestor *Australopithecus africanus*, then newly discovered in the arid fringe country of the Kalahari desert:

> 'In anticipating the discovery of the true links between the apes and man in tropical countries, there has been a tendency to overlook the fact that, in the luxuriant forests of the tropical belts, Nature was supplying with profligate and lavish hand an easy and sluggish solution, by adaptive specialization, of the problem of existence in creatures so well equipped mentally as living anthropoids are. For the production of man a different apprenticeship was needed to sharpen the wits and quicken the higher manifestations of intellect – a more open veldt country where competition was keener between swiftness and stealth, and where adroitness of thinking and movement played a preponderating role in the preservation of the species . . . South Africa, by providing a vast, open country with occasional wooded belts and a relative scarcity of water, together with a fierce and bitter mammalian competition, furnished a laboratory such as was essential to this penultimate phase of human evolution.'

Man is related to the great apes, ran the classical reasoning, and the great apes live in the lush tropical forests; therefore man must have originated in the tropical forests. Dart's insight was that, of all the possibilities, this was the least likely; if man had begun as a tropical forest ape then that is what he would be now. Clearly there had been something different in man's history, or he would now be no more than another struggling, declining chimpanzee or orang-outang, clinging desperately to his hospitable, shrinking forests. But precisely because of the difference in his history, he is now ruling the earth. For he was thrown into the hostile world of the savannah and the grassland, of the lion and the leopard, where there were neither fruits on the bough nor highways through the treetops. And man, in one of the most dazzling of evolution's many extraordinary achievements, in the first instance survived, and in the second instance dominated, his mean and unfriendly surroundings. He had no choice; it was either that or go under; and against all the odds he did not go under.

What has happened since those far-off days on the African veld, so eloquently recreated by Robert Ardrey,[8] has been merely an extension of, not a fundamental change in, man's interaction with his environment. He survived then because he dominated the physical world he lived in; we have taken up where he left off and extended, broadened and deepened the domination process. When he first seized an antelope's humerus and brought it crashing down on a baboon's skull, he was doing in his way what we do in ours, when we develop a new pesticide or antibiotic, build a power station, construct a jet airliner, or drop an atomic bomb. Should we not at least be consistent? – if we are to say to the australopithecine, 'Well done, my boy: you triumphed against mighty odds', must we not also say to ourselves, 'If only the australopithecines could see us now, how proud they would be'? We have taken their charter and fulfilled it to the utmost of our endeavour; we have completed what they began; and how can we now label this *failure* in any conceivable sense of the word?

Truly, 'we have never had it so good'. (I write, of course, as a child of the technocratic, developed Western world; I cannot speak for the majority of mankind, the undeveloped nations.) Diseases threatened us, and we first controlled and later conquered them; food was hard to come by and we increased, manyfold, the productivity of the earth. We were cold, and we created warmth; we were weak, and we created power; we were slow, and we created speed. Since our watchword, like that of every organic being, was and is 'Survive for today and reproduce for tomorrow', who will say that we have not achieved our goal with quite unparalleled success?

Of course we are now finding that our strategy has some disadvantages to it; but then what strategy doesn't? Certainly we can advocate a 'return to nature', as long as we are perfectly clear about what we mean by it. Capping this smokestack and conserving that forest are undoubtedly good, clean, healthy things to do; but they are not in themselves relevant to the question of man's survival. The choice facing us is whether or not we are going to perpetuate the human way of life; and inevitably, therefore, it is a non-choice. Would it have been a choice if we had said to Shakespeare, 'You really must stop writing all this stuff; you're using up a fearful lot of paper'? Of course not: use of vast quantities of paper was a price it would have been absurd not to pay for what Shakespeare was giving us. And we are now being told that the drama of man is a washout and we must rethink everything we have written: is it any wonder that we are refusing to accept the diagnosis?

The whole point about humanity is that it is humane. We can feed the starving, we can cure the sick, we can comfort the wretched; we can rise above the law of the jungle and the decimation of the unfit; that is where humanity began and that is where it will end. Why should we feel guilty about it, or castigate ourselves because it has happened, or weep for what might have been? We have reached the summit, and perhaps the view isn't quite as spectacular as we had hoped it would be, but it's still a hell of a lot better than the view from the plain beneath.

And so today's crusading student becomes tomorrow's suburban conservative, driving one of those evil and destructive motor cars, using vast quantities of electrical power in his cleaner-than-clean home, having as many children as he pleases. Why should we be surprised, or indignant, or unhappy? He is merely surviving by the set of values man has always survived by and, whatever you might think, you can hardly deny him that right, or suggest that he should try anything else. He is a member of the last generation, and he has every reason to be proud, and unrepentant, and grateful for it. The rest of the book is no more than an amplification of this circumstance, of how our situation has come about and where it is leading us to.

NOTES

1 EHRLICH, PAUL R. *The Population Bomb* (London, Ballantine Books 1971)
2 BRIERLEY, J. K. *Biology and the Social Crisis* (London, Heinemann Educational Books, 1967)
3 DYLAN, BOB. 'Blowin' in the Wind', quoted in Antony Scaduto, *Dylan* (London, W. H. Allen 1972)
4 HARDIN, GARRETT. 'The Tragedy of the Commons', *Science,* Vol. 162 (1968), 1243-48
5 BOULDING, KENNETH E. 'The Economics of the Coming Spaceship Earth', in: Garrett Hardin (ed.) *Population, Evolution and Birth Control*. (Reading, W. H. Freeman 1969)
6 MARTIN, ANGUS. *Pollution and Conservation in Australia* (Melbourne, Lansdowne Press 1971)
7 DART, RAYMOND A. '*Australopithecus africanus*: The Man-Ape of South Africa', *Nature*, Vol. 115 (1925) 195–199
8 ARDREY, ROBERT. *African Genesis* (London, Collins 1961)

2 The Dog Beneath the Skin

'Drinking when we are not thirsty and making love at
all seasons, madam: that is all there is to distinguish us
from the other animals.'

de Beaumarchais: *The Marriage of Figaro*

In order to show my true colours from the beginning I shall
start with a highly unoriginal statement; one that has been
rammed down our throats in a hundred different ways, rang-
ing from the ingenious speculations of Desmond Morris[1]
through the purple prose of Robert Ardrey[2] to the abstruse
ramblings of Arthur Koestler:[3] *Man is an animal*. The statement is worth repeating. Its significance lies not in the fact
that it reminds us of our flesh-and-blood, brain-and-brawn,
hormone-and-nerve constitution; rather it means: Man, like
every member of the animal kingdom, is a product of the
process of organic evolution. That, too, is a fairly obvious
thing to say: what are not so obvious are its implications.
While we have been uncovering increasingly complete evidence of the physical stages through which man's descent
has come, the interpretation of the causes behind those
changes has lagged far behind. Even today there is an extraordinarily large quantity of pseudo-evolutionary writing
being poured out, much of it achieving wide currency and
acclaim not only from the lay reviewer but from parts of the
scientific community itself. An odd state of affairs, but an
explicable one: it could even be said to follow a pattern
which is inevitable given a particular set of circumstances.
These are: (*i*) a relatively new and complex science which is
an utter mystery to the layman; (*ii*) an enthusiastic lay re-

searcher; and (*iii*) (as a result of his researches) a popular book which explains the mystery. A case history: (*i*) the new and frightening world of the nuclear physicists and the atomic bomb; (*ii*) Robert Jungk; and (*iii*) *Brighter than a Thousand Suns*.[4] Suddenly there is light (and not only the light of the thousand suns); the layman is put in the picture and stands in grateful awe of the man who was able to reduce such a diabolically intricate business to a level he could understand. Later, after the popularizer has done his job and achieved enormous influence, come the professional physicists who point out that *Brighter than a Thousand Suns* 'is marred by inaccuracies on nearly every page . . . Jungk has not gone sufficiently deep to acquire the understanding necessary to qualify him for the kind of analysis he attempts . . . Jungk's subject is too big for him; his conclusions are frequently irresponsible, sensational and in questionable taste . . . Jungk's profound errors of judgement . . . his lighthearted and uncritical approach towards his material . . .'[5] and so on. But by then, of course, the damage is done; the popular book is readable, exciting, believable; the professionals, by comparison, are distant, uninteresting and distinctly sour-grapesish.

All this has happened to the story of human evolution, too, but it has gone even deeper: the popularizer has, in many cases, convinced even the professionals. There are probably scores of reasons why this should be so; we can, I think, identify the most important ones. The most outstanding is undoubtedly the fact that evolution is an exceedingly complicated concept when it is looked at *in toto*. Virtually anyone can readily grasp the simple cause-and-effect logic behind the case of the English peppered moths which were replaced by black ones in industrial areas. Such concepts as adaptation and the survival of the fittest, at least in principle, have a fine, commonsensical air about them; it doesn't seem to require any special expertise to understand them. Any biologist working on an evolutionary problem will be able to explain to you approximately what he is doing and how it fits in with the overall story of organic evolution. Any reasonably intelligent person can, it seems, quickly become an evolutionary home handyman; he may lack the finesse of the true craftsman, but he gets there in the end just the same.

Unfortunately, when it comes to the interpretation of the major questions of evolution, the home handyman approach is simply not good enough. Common sense is not just a poor guide: it is the vandal who comes in the night and turns all the signposts around. A concept may have a feeling of rightness about it, a measure of both emotional and logical appeal, but that doesn't mean a damned thing. For an already well-aired example one has to look no further than the inheritance of acquired characteristics, a concept which seemed reasonable enough and which had enormous appeal. The first nails were driven firmly into the lid of its coffin as early as 1896, and yet that did not prevent the extraordinary spectacle of an eminent nation hitching its wagon to this superficially bright, but inwardly shabby, star. Under the name of Lysenkoism it held sway in the Soviet Union from approximately 1936 to 1964.[6] And even in 1971 Arthur Koestler found it necessary to present a spirited defence of the concept as part of his study of one of its more notorious disciples, Paul Kammerer.[7]

There are several other weeds which have taken firm root and blossomed among the evolutionary crop; indeed, an unbelievably large amount of non-evolutionary philosophy has appeared in the guise of evolution since the days of the giants: Darwin, Thomas Huxley, R. A. Fisher. None, perhaps, has had the impact of neo-Lamarckism, but in these days of endless quest after panaceas for the human predicament, man's animal nature is being aired in discussion with increasing frequency: sometimes, oddly enough, as a whipping-boy for all our troubles; at other times as a solution to them.

Consider, for instance, the proposition advanced by Konrad Lorenz in *On Aggression*: Man is the only animal which lacks built-in inhibitions with regard to killing his own kind.[8] A compellingly attractive idea: it explains in a flash man's almost unique propensity for waging wars and killing vast numbers of his species in the process. It is even backed by a plausible evolutionary explanation: most potentially dangerous animals have evolved with their weaponry (fangs, talons, claws, horns) over long periods of time. They have therefore had the opportunity to evolve inhibitions about using their weapons on members of their own species, which (if it happened) clearly would not be for the 'good of the species'. Man, by contrast, invented his weapons only a few hundred thousand years ago; he did not evolve with them all along the way; he was basically a harmless vegetarian who was physically incapable of seriously damaging his compatriots. Hence, no need for inhibitions about killing, and when he suddenly found himself possessed of lethal armaments – sticks, stones, arrows, bullets, hydrogen bombs – he had the potential to kill and lacked the restraint system to control it. *Ergo*, he kills.

Lorenz is an ethologist, perhaps the greatest ever student of animal behaviour, and that is what he says about aggression and killing in man. But he isn't alone. Anthony Storr, a psychiatrist, says the same thing.[9] So does Robert Ardrey, the prophet of pop anthropology.[10] So does Sir Macfarlane Burnet, a Nobel-prize-winning medical scientist.[11] And Harrison Matthews, a prominent British zoologist.[12] And so on.

There are grounds enough for suspicion here: the hypothesis is appealing, commonsensical, and it has the backing of both scientists and prominent laymen. What is wrong with it, not to put too fine a point upon it, is that it is anti-evolutionary. Such a system could not be produced by the mechanisms of natural selection. Charles Fort, an inspired and witty doubter of all things scientific, was reacting in similar vein to the phenomenon of water divining when he wrote: 'Now there are so many scientists who believe in dowsing that the suspicion comes to me that it may be only a myth after all.'[13] No doubt he would have had much the same feelings about the man-is-an-animal philosophy now that (in some quarters, at least) it is becoming scientifically respectable.

Of course there are explanations in terms of man's evolutionary history for his current behaviour. But they frequently aren't particularly appealing, logically, emotionally, or commonsensically. We tend to automatically reject them, using our highly-developed hear-no-evil, see-no-evil, smell-no-evil peripheral filter. *Thou shalt not kill*, for instance, obviously means simply that it is wrong to kill your fellow man. Or that is what church, law, and society tell us, anyway. But, as Robert Bigelow[14] has pointed out, that is clearly not what Moses meant by it. When he said it, it meant: Thou shalt not kill *fellow Israelites*. Equally, he might have said: 'It's a dashed good idea to kill Canaanites and all those other foreign scum, but don't start getting carried away and kill one of us.' Neighbour, likewise, meant fellow-tribesman, and all of the business about not stealing and not coveting wives and oxen and other household necessities applied strictly to members of your own tribe; anyone else was fair game.

What happened in 1953 when Raymond Dart[15] suggested in a scientific paper that our phylogenetic ancestors, the australopithecines, were weapon-wielding, bloodthirsty carnivores? The editor of the journal in which the paper appeared found it necessary to add a note at the end of the paper, to the effect that these creatures were the ancestors of the 'modern bushman and Negro, and of *nobody else*'; that 'this carnivorous stage may have been very short for some of the European races (who go back to different ape-ancestors)';

and that modern man shows 'intolerance to meat eating' and 'suffers from many diseases which immediately disappear under a vegetarian diet'. And what do we do when Paul Ehrlich talks about millions of people starving to death? We picture malnourished Indians.

The truth is the hardest thing of all to bear. Evolutionary truths are no exception, and the true implications of our animal nature for the problems of overpopulation, pollution, quality of life, and all the rest of it, are not particularly comforting ones.

In 1943 David Lack,[16] a modern evolutionary giant if ever there was one, said a remarkably nasty thing: that the average life span in the wild of that familiar and engaging creature, the English robin, was about eighteen months. On the face of it an absurd statement to make; why, in captivity robins have lived for more like eighteen years. But Lack had the facts and the figures (he even records, in a section on causes of death, the cases of two robins which choked on a horsehair and another which got its head stuck between two slats in a fence), and the most ardent bird-lover had to grudgingly admit that he was right. Now here is a clue about man from the animal world: no wild robin ever dies of old age. And many, many men do. Surely somewhere in there must be lurking a moral for us.

What do robins die of? Apart from accidents with horsehairs and fences: cats, rats, dogs, stoats, weasels and owls eat them, cars run them over, mousetraps catch them, they freeze to death, and they starve. If you knew personally one hundred adult robins and one hundred juveniles on 1 August in any year, on 31 July in the next year only thirty-eight of your adult acquaintances and twenty-eight of the youngsters would still be alive. The great majority of the rest would have starved to death during the winter. A further remarkable fact is that the population density of robins in any given area remains fairly constant from year to year; the robin is not, as the mortality figures might suggest, heading for extinction. This means, obviously enough, that each pair of parent robins must be just replacing itself. For each two adults that die two recruits must be entering the population: there is no other way of achieving a stable population size. But how do they manage to replace themselves if seventy-two per cent of young robins die in their first year? Each pair lays, on the average, ten eggs in a year (in two clutches of five), and, allowing for the eggs which fail to hatch and the nestlings which die, you can easily calculate that only two reproducing adults will eventually result from each batch of ten eggs.

Thus we have a perfectly straightforward explanation for the fact that, although a pair of robins produces ten offspring in a year (i.e. potentially replaces itself fivefold), a robin population explosion does not occur. As a working hypothesis we could assume that each robin is reproducing as hard as it can go – flogging its guts out, we might say – and by so doing it just manages to replace itself. It produces as many offspring as it possibly can, but predators, diseases, climatic hazards and food shortage claim most of them before they are mature. In equation form:

Overproduction + Heavy Mortality = Population Control.

Now this reasoning becomes virtually self-evident when one recalls what natural selection is all about. Individuals vary; many of the variations are hereditary; and some variants reproduce more successfully than others. Those which produce the greater numbers of offspring provide a greater proportion of the subsequent generation; their genetic constitution is being selected *for*. An individual which leaves fewer offspring (or none at all) will be selected *against*. It follows that the evolutionary rule which every organism is governed by is: *Leave as many offspring as you possibly can.*

There is always the chance that some of your overproduction will survive; if you do not follow the rule there is no chance whatever, and your lineage will be reaped by the scythe of natural selection.

But . . . (there is always a but). We are assuming that a clutch of five is the greatest that a robin can possibly manage. But clutches of six and seven are known; more rarely clutches of eight to twelve. In 1944, history records, a robin laid a clutch of twenty. We must grant that that is exceptional, but there are enough clutches of ten on record to show that plenty of robins are perfectly capable of laying ten eggs in a clutch (i.e. twenty in a year), but the vast majority lay only five (ten for the year). Our gut-flogging hypothesis is starting to look a little shaky; if the bird is laying only half the clutch it is capable of then it is obviously not reproducing as hard as it can go. It seems as though it may be practising a form of birth control; we could write another equation:

Limit on Number of Births=Just Enough Production to Maintain Population=Population Control.

Perhaps that is the sort of thing that robins are striving to achieve?

It was observations of this sort which led the British biologist V. C. Wynne-Edwards to propose a revolutionary theory of population regulation in animals: *Animal Dispersion in Relation to Social Behaviour*, published in 1962.[17] The orthodox theory up to that time was something like our equation (1) above:

Overproduction+Heavy Mortality=Population Control.

Whatever else this equation may be, it is certainly not pleasant; it is not even logical. Why produce all those offspring if they're only going to die? It's downright wasteful: the whole business sounds thoroughly messy and inefficient.

Wynne-Edwards' alternative theory has a great many ramifications to it, but in essence it is delightfully simple. It suggests that there is a variety of mechanisms by which animal populations prevent themselves from outstripping their food supply. Deliberately limiting their clutch (or litter) size is one. This, in the jargon of the theory, is 'prudential restraint'. The reproductively-ready pair, in effect, have a look around before they begin to procreate. If the population is sparse, well and good. But if it is booming; if food is low or getting low, then it is prudent not to breed – it is prudent to show restraint. So some pairs do not breed, even though they are physiologically capable of it.

Territoriality is another of these population-limiting mechanisms. If there are twenty acres of land and each individual requires only enough space to stand up in (say one square foot), then about 900,000 individuals will be able to fit into the area (and utterly denude it of food in no time at all). But if each individual has an exclusive territory of half an acre, then, willy-nilly, you can fit only forty individuals in. The population of the area is limited; the available food is not overtaxed. Further, non-territory-holders will not breed; this, like prudential restraint, represents another form of birth control.

Now here is a theory which appears to make more sense. No wastage, no excessive mortality; instead a neat feedback loop which regulates the birth rate and prevents over-exploitation of food and other resources. Appealing? Yes. Common sense? Decidedly. Distinguished adherents? Plenty . . . J. le Gay Brereton.[18] Bernard Campbell.[19] Arthur Koestler.[20] Robert Ardrey.[21]

You should, by now, be highly suspicious. We have all the ingredients here of another of those Great Evolutionary Impostors, the non-evolutionary wolf in the Darwinian sheep's clothing. And of course you are right. Think again about the way in which natural selection operates. The successful individual (or, using jargon again, the *fittest* individual) is he who leaves most offspring. An individual who practises prudential restraint is thereby ensuring that he leaves fewer offspring than one who doesn't. The prudent individual is being selected against; the genetic constitution he carries will disappear from the population. Prudential restraint is simply not possible.

(As Garrett Hardin[22] has pointed out, conscience [or the 'sense of responsibility'] in man is similarly self-eliminating in regard to the question of family size. If you appeal to people's consciences – 'Now, now, be good chaps and show some restraint' – some people will heed you and some will not. Those who do not will outbreed those who do; conscience will, in the long term, be selected out of the population.)

But what of the robin which lays only five eggs, when we know perfectly well that it could lay ten if it wanted to? That proves, surely, that it is *not* producing the maximum possible number of offspring. But hold hard: let's define what we mean by *offspring*.

Take two creatures. One lays a thousand eggs and the other ten. Which has had more offspring? The first. Of the thousand eggs three hundred hatch; of the ten, nine hatch. Which has had more? Still the first. Of the three hundred four survive to adulthood; of the nine, eight reach maturity. Which has had more offspring? The *second*. Offspring, in the evolutionary sense, are those descendants which survive to an age when they can reproduce. If you have a million offspring all of whom die before puberty you have achieved precisely nothing. If you have one offspring which reaches adulthood you have achieved a great deal.

Let's have a second look at this matter of clutch size in birds. Christopher Perrins,[23] a student of David Lack, carried out an elegant little experiment on European swifts. This bird normally lays clutches of two or three eggs in

England, rarely four. But it can lay four. Why doesn't it always? Perrins artificially augmented some clutches in a total of 108, so that he ended up with seventy-two clutches of two, twenty clutches of three, and sixteen clutches of four eggs. The work was spread over four years and included good seasons and bad. The critical step in the experiment was to count the number of young actually reared from clutches of two, three, and four eggs. And what he found was this: the mean number of young raised from a clutch of two was 1.95. From a clutch of three: 2.59. And from a clutch of four: 1.84.

That is a rather complete answer to the problem. Swifts can lay four eggs, yes; but they cannot raise four young. Clutches of four actually result in *fewer* surviving offspring than do clutches of two or three. And evolutionary fitness is measured not in the number of eggs laid, but in the number of young raised from those eggs. Each pair of swifts is producing the maximum number of offspring that it is capable of raising.

But (you may be objecting, quite rightly), in that case why do so many swifts lay clutches of only two? Perrins had thought of that, too. In a season of plenty it is not especially difficult to raise three young, but in a lean year it is just about impossible. In a poor summer clutches of three have a mean success of 1.5 or so; clutches of two, about 1.8. Hence both two-egg and three-egg lineages persist in the population; in lean years one is favoured and in fat years the other. And of course there will be the rare exceptionally bountiful season when it is possible to rear four young swifts; hence the persistence of four-egg lineages.

A brief comment on Wynne-Edwards' interpretation of territoriality. It would work if territories were of a fixed size, but obviously if territories can be compressed then a finite area need not impose an absolute limit on the number of residents it can contain. Lack's robins held territories varying in size from only half an acre to more than two acres; song-thrush territories vary from 3.75 to 14.75 acres.[24] If this is a limit then it's a highly flexible one.

There are other, and more serious, objections to Wynne-Edwards' ideas, but we shall return to them later. For the moment we shall instead review what we have learned from Lack's robins and Perrins' swifts, and see how much it tells us about the problems of population growth and regulation in another animal species, *Homo sapiens*.

We must of course take as our starting assumption, both by analogy with the birds and by virtue of the mechanism of action of natural selection, that man reproduces as fast as he can. From this it follows that man is subject to our first equation:

Overproduction+Heavy Mortality=Population Control.
Since this is clearly nonsense if we try to apply it to modern man (whose populations are not controlled), we shall have to go back in time, and examine the situation prior to the development of agriculture — say twenty or thirty thousand years ago.

But first: what is man's average litter (or family) size? Or rather, if each pair did try to reproduce as hard as it could, how many children would it have? A modern estimated mean is eight, which is derived from a female reproductive span of twenty years with a child every 2.5 years (this interval allows for some miscarriages and temporary sterility). Since the maximum life span twenty thousand years ago was of the order of thirty years (and this is something that has increased only very recently; some estimates are: Greece, 400 BC — 30 years; Rome, AD 600 — 30 years; England, AD 800 — 31 years; England, 1450 — 33 years; England, 1815 — 39 years),[25] a more reasonable total fertility estimate would be four children. This is still enough to replace the parents twice

L.G.   B over, and yet we know that the population explosion did not really get under way until the late seventeenth century. What happened to the extra two children?

They died, obviously. E. S. Deevey[26] estimates that in pre-agricultural man, child mortality may have been as high as one in two (in modern demographic terms, because there are so many more of us, this would be expressed as 500 in 1,000 or 500/1,000.) Merely to replace themselves a couple *had* to have four children.

What did the children die of? Starvation, mainly, but also predation, natural disasters, war, and disease. Joseph Birdsell's[27] fascinating studies of the Australian Aboriginals (as a sort of model of what early hunter-gatherer communities may have been like) revealed two very interesting things: most tribes numbered about five hundred individuals, and there was a close correlation between size of tribal area and rainfall. Since productivity is also closely tied to rainfall we can deduce that tribal size was limited by food availability. If a tribe grew much larger than five hundred it was rapidly cut back to size by starvation of the excess numbers. A. H. Hawley[28] writes: 'Isolated populations live close to the brink of catastrophe at all times. That is indicated by their high average death rates and life expectancies of about thirty years or less. The margin of safety is sometimes so small that a decline of but a few inches in the annual rainfall or the loss of a few days from the normal growing season is sufficient to produce widespread suffering and loss of life.' A typical example of the workings of our Equation One – no matter how hard the members of the tribe worked at reproduction it was almost impossible to achieve an increase in numbers. They had to run as fast as they could merely to stay in the same place.

You may well query this. But, you may say, we know very well that deliberate birth control is almost as old as human history. J. S. Weiner[29] tells us that in 'simple societies . . . (like many animal societies) stability of numbers is in fact aimed at and more or less achieved'. (I hope your immediate reaction to that is to say, 'Oh yeah? What animal societies?') F. le Gros Clark[30] writes, 'So-called tribal society men . . . tended to limit the growth of numbers by such crude but effective checks as abortion, infanticide, perpetual widowhood, and taboos upon cohabitation over certain seasons'. And there are Egyptian papyri dating from 1900 BC which show that their writers had a clear knowledge of contraceptive techniques.[31]

Have we forgotten the lesson of clutch size in robins and swifts already? Swifts lay clutches of three eggs when they could lay clutches of four: are they aiming at and achieving stability of numbers by controlling the birth rate? Of course not; they're trying to *maximize numbers*. They achieve larger, not smaller, families by laying three instead of four eggs. And so it was with humans. Imagine a Palaeolithic woman with an eighteen-month-old child; she then has another baby. (The situation in man is complicated by the long gestation period. The second child may have been conceived in a time of plenty but arrive in a time of want.) Drought strikes. What is she to do? Should she share the meagre resources between the two and in all probability lose both? Wouldn't it be better to abandon the second and concentrate on the first, which has already had eighteen months of sweat and toil invested in it? Which will maximize her family size?

Note that in times of famine the earlier she terminated the second pregnancy the better off she would be. Hence there would have been enormous rewards, in terms of maximizing population growth, for groups which learned the techniques of abortion to replace infanticide, contraception to replace or supplement abortion. Note also that in times of real crises the most efficient and sensible thing would have been to use the second child as food for the first. (John Wyndham,[32] interestingly enough, arrives at basically this conclusion when dealing with a group of people marooned in a spaceship, in *Survival*, a short story set at some undefined time in the future.) Cannibalism among men has a long and respectable history, going back at least as far as Solo Man in Java (100,000 or so years ago).[33] All we have of Solo Man is two bits of leg and eleven skulls; and every skull has had the whole face and floor smashed out. The Solo River was clearly the site of a stupendous brain-feast. (Ashley Montagu, on the other hand, by analogy with a practice of an Aboriginal tribe in South Australia, suggests that the skulls may have been used as drinking vessels.[34] As he quite reasonably points out, 'Java is . . . very near Australia'. Since the Aborigines in question lived in extreme southern Australia, 'very near' is almost 3,000 miles as the crow flies.)

Another point about infant mortality has probably struck you by this time. If, as we are assuming, man is operating on the principle of having as many offspring as possible, why haven't multiple births become more firmly established by natural selection? If a modern woman had quads at every confinement her total fertility would be not eight but thirty-two: now there's maximizing family size for you! But the frequency of twins is only about one birth in ninety; of triplets and so on even less. Why? Because, in a hunting and gathering (or even primitive agricultural) community, it's hard enough for a mother to rear one child at a time, let alone two or three. Twinning, until very recently, must have been severely selected against; and in countless primitive societies one of each pair of twins was (or is) killed very shortly after birth.

Even not having a child at some particular times is a way of increasing family size. It would be disastrous to become pregnant during a time of extreme hardship; the probability of survival of a pregnant woman would be considerably less than that of a non-pregnant one. Infinitely better to bide your time for a few months or years, and have your child when there was a reasonable chance of rearing it. One can easily appreciate the enormous selective value there would have been in being able to judge the likely productivity of particular places and seasons.

But this, you may be saying, is no more nor less than good old prudential restraint! Which of course it is, in the literal sense, but not Wynne-Edwards' sense, of the phrase. His concept of prudential restraint is that it is a mechanism which lowers the birth rate of some individuals in order to increase the probability of survival of the population, or at least part of the population, to which they belong. Thus individual goals, desires, benefits, fitness, or whatever, are sacrificed for the common good. We can envisage populations which contain prudent, self-sacrificing individuals, and which survive; and other populations which lack such individuals and die. We shall look in the next chapter at the manner in which all this is supposed to come about.

All we need note for now is that none of this need concern us in arguments about the human situation. In man, deliberate birth control (or 'prudential restraint' if you insist) has clearly arisen as an *individual* means of *maximizing* family size; we do not need to worry about self-sacrifice or the common good. Since birth control arose purely and simply as a means of increasing reproductive success, of increasing fitness, it is explicable – it could be said to be inevitable – in terms of straightforward natural selection theory.

It is also worth noting a couple of other unusual things about man's reproductive biology. One is his long reproductive life span: refraining from reproduction in one year may increase the likelihood of successful procreation in the next year, or the next, or the next . . . Shorter-lived creatures do not have this flexibility. Secondly, man is equipped with the ability to make reasonably accurate short-term forecasts, based on probability scales derived from past experience. This capacity derives largely from his elegant system of cultural information transmission and storage; a facility not possessed by any other creature to even a fraction of the same extent.

The story of human populations since the agricultural revolution is purely and simply a history of the decreasing applicability of Equation One to them. Mortality rates remained high after the advent of agriculture; nevertheless the ratio of birth rate to death rate slowly began to alter. Food ceased to be a day-to-day crisis but horrifying famines still occurred. The population of Ireland when potatoes were introduced from the New World in 1754 was 3.2 million. By 1846 this had more than doubled, to 8.2 million; then the potato blight struck. By 1871 the population had been cut back (by mortality and emigration) to 4 million.[35]

Even more horrifying were the huge outbreaks of epidemic disease which raged through the Middle Ages and into the latter part of the last century. The Black Death of 1348-50 (a combination of bubonic, pneumonic and septicaemic plagues) killed 20 million people in Europe out of a total population of 85 million. It took until the middle of the sixteenth century for the population of Europe to recover to its level of 1347.[36] There was almost nothing that could be done to reduce the mortality resulting from infectious diseases; in the crowded, insanitary cities they travelled like wildfire. An outbreak of cholera arrived in London in June 1849; there were 250 deaths in that month, 2,000 in July, 4,000 in August and 7,000 in September.[37] For further examples of the toll that typhus and other diseases have exacted in the not-too-distant past Hans Zinsser's wise and witty *Rats, Lice and History*[38] should be consulted.

We may also note that late marriage,* enforced celibacy, and infanticide were extremely significant checks to population growth during this period. W. L. Langer[39] provides an account of the operation of these factors in Europe in the eighteenth and nineteenth centuries; a period during which Europe's population doubled, but could theoretically have achieved a much higher growth rate. Landowners were both willing and able to control the size of the population resident on their land; one common way of doing it was to forbid servants and tenants to marry (and defiance meant certain eviction). In parts of Germany most young men were conscripted into the army for a term of at least six years; young women became household servants; and housing for poor people was intentionally kept in short supply. Again, in Würtemburg in 1712 laws were passed forbidding marriage to any man who could not prove that he could support a wife.

Even if poor people did have children (illegitimately) they could usually not afford to keep them. There was an easy way out: infanticide. The methods varied: overdoses of gin or narcotics, strangulation, asphyxiation and starvation were all popular. Even easier was simple abandonment, in essence also infanticide, since foundlings who ended up in the workhouses and hospitals rarely lived to tell the tale. In the years 1756–59 fifteen thousand infants were taken in by the London Foundling Hospital; less than a third of them survived to adolescence. Between 1728 and 1757 less than forty per cent of abandoned infants in England reached the age even of two. In France in 1811 Napoleon caused laws to be passed which

---

* If couples in one population produce four children by the age of twenty, and couples in another (of equal initial size) four children by the age of thirty, then after sixty years the former population will be twice the size of the latter.

made the disposal of babies so easy and anonymous that it is likely that thousands of *legitimate* children were consigned to hospices – which for most of them was a death sentence.

Basically it is obvious that all this was a direct consequence of the haves making sure that their position of dominance was not threatened by the have-nots. They held the whip hand; food was so scarce that if a pauper lost his position or suffered eviction his plight was serious indeed. What eventually relaxed the landlords' stranglehold was the introduction from the New World in the mid-eighteenth century of two nutritious, easily-grown crops: maize and potatoes. As we have seen from the Irish example, this had an enormous influence. Now even the poorest family could cultivate a potato patch and raise half a dozen children; it is estimated that the food supply to even the most destitute of people increased by twenty-five to thirty per cent. Added to which, of course, were the Industrial Revolution and the opportunity to emigrate to the New World; the spectre of overpopulation in Europe seemed at last to be allayed.

Hence it is not surprising to find that it was about this time that Equation One began to undergo a transformation, so that it now came to read:

Overproduction+Sharply Declining Mortality=
$$\text{Uncontrolled Population Growth.}$$

Note that the first term in the equation remains unaltered. There has not been any noticeable increase in the birthrate; indeed, in many parts of the world there has been a decrease. All that has changed is the mortality factor: a greater proportion of babies are surviving to become reproducing adults than ever before. If our robins and swifts were to be provided with food and shelter during the winter then exactly the same thing would happen to them (and in fact does happen in cities, where the birds can avail themselves of human help to temper the severity of winter). We have managed to alter the second term in the equation; they have not: and that is the only fundamental difference between their population biology and ours. For rural robins the birth and death rates were undoubtedly much the same in 1930 as they were in 1969; but for Mexicans a 1930 birth rate of 45/1,000 and death rate of 27/1,000 had been replaced by a birth rate of 43/1,000 and a death rate of 10/1,000 by 1969.[40]

Of course Equation One is an instance of that class of natural phenomena, like the necessity to eat and the velocity of light, about which Science must regretfully admit that there is nothing it can do in a permanent way. The transformation of Equation One was only a very temporary affair; already it is reverting at an accelerating pace to its old form. Given a finite earth with finite resources there is no other outcome possible. We are living on borrowed time, and our creditors are starting to get a little impatient. Even the Western nations' stratagem of living at the expense of the undeveloped world has now achieved nearly all the postponement it is capable of. All that Paul Ehrlich is doing is to point out what should be self-evident: the *Declining Mortality* term in our equation has begun to be replaced by a new term, *Hundreds of millions of people will starve to death*.

It may be objected at this point that I have forgotten the demographic transition: the drop in the birthrate that has followed industrialization in most countries. In Sweden the death rate dropped from 20/1,000 in 1860 to 10/1,000 in 1960; in the same period the birth rate dropped from 34/1,000 to 15/1,000. In other words a growth rate of 1.4% fell to one of 0.5% in a century.[40]

No, I have not forgotten about it; I just do not see that it is particularly relevant to the problem. The Western world is already grossly overpopulated, particularly in terms of its resource requirements; and populations are still growing.

Growing more slowly, certainly, but growing all the same. Further, we do not really understand why the demographic transition occurs, but we do know that it follows industrialization. And the Third World, of course, will never be industrialized in the manner of Europe or the USA – it is probably not desirable; it is certainly not possible. It is not going to have a demographic transition in the foreseeable future. A demographic transition has happened to less than a third of the world's population: wouldn't it be wiser to view the other two thirds as more representative of the true situation?

Man is an animal. Perhaps we can now appreciate more fully the significance of that statement. Population growth in man stems from two factors. One (which he shares with all other animals) is that natural selection favours the individuals who rear the most offspring: those who achieve the greatest overproduction. The second, which is unique to him, is that his overproduction lives and reproduces because of his temporary control of mortality rates. The rest of the story is merely one of waiting for mortality to catch up.

It's as simple as that. When Robert Ardrey[21] writes 'any population, human or non-human, has within its powers the limitation of numbers through conventional rules and regulations and the capacity to abide by them' and 'birth control . . . is a cultural substitute for biological mechanisms prevalent in the natural world', we can only wonder at man's uncanny talent for transforming straightforward issues into contorted rigmaroles. Or consider this statement by Wynne-Edwards:[41] 'lacking the built-in homeostatic system that regulates the density of animal populations, man cannot look to any natural process to restrain his rapid growth'. I would that were true. But unfortunately one of the oldest and most natural processes known has already begun to flex its muscles: Starvation. *The battle to feed all of humanity is over . . . hundreds of millions of people will starve to death.*

NOTES

1 MORRIS, DESMOND. *The Naked Ape* (London, Jonathan Cape 1967)

2 ARDREY, ROBERT. *African Genesis* (London, Collins 1961) ARDREY, ROBERT. *The Territorial Imperative* (London, Collins 1967)

3 KOESTLER, ARTHUR. *The Ghost in the Machine* (London, Hutchinson 1967)

4 JUNGK, ROBERT. *Brighter than a Thousand Suns* (London, Gollancz and Hart-Davis 1958).

5 WILSON, ROBERT R. 1958. 'The Scientists Who Made the Atom Bomb', in: Garrett Hardin (ed.) *Science, Conflict and Society* (Reading, W. H. Freeman 1969)

6 LERNER, I. MICHAEL. *Heredity, Evolution and Society* (Reading, W. H. Freeman 1968)

7 KOESTLER, ARTHUR. *The Case of the Midwife Toad* (London, Hutchinson 1971)

8 LORENZ, KONRAD. *On Aggression* (London, Methuen 1966)

9 STORR, ANTHONY. *Human Aggression* (London, Allen Lane: The Penguin Press 1968)

10 ARDREY, ROBERT. *The Territorial Imperative* (London, Collins 1967)

11 BURNET, MACFARLANE. *Dominant Mammal* (London, Heinemann 1970)

12 MATTHEWS, L. HARRISON. 'Overt Fighting in Mammals', in: J. D. Carthy and F. J. Ebling (eds.) *The Natural History of Aggression* (London, Academic Press 1964)

13 FORT, CHARLES. Quoted by GARDNER, MARTIN, in *Fads and Fallacies in the Name of Science* (New York, Dover Books 1957)

14 BIGELOW, ROBERT. *The Dawn Warriors* (London, Hutchinson 1969)

15 DART, RAYMOND A. 'The Predatory Transition from Ape to Man', *International Anthropological and Linguistic Review*, Vol. 1 (1953) 210–18

16 LACK, DAVID. *The Life of the Robin* (London, Collins 1943)

17 WYNNE-EDWARDS, V. C. *Animal Dispersion in Relation to Social Behaviour* (Edinburgh, Oliver and Boyd 1962)

18 BRERETON, J. LE G. 'Evolved Regulatory Mechanisms of Population Control', in: G. W. Leeper (ed.) *The Evolution of Living Organisms* (Melbourne University Press 1961)

19 CAMPBELL, BERNARD. *Human Evolution* (London, Heinemann Educational Books 1966)

20 KOESTLER, ARTHUR. *The Ghost in the Machine* (London, Hutchinson 1967)

21 ARDREY, ROBERT. *The Social Contract* (London, Collins 1970)

22 HARDIN, GARRETT. 'The Tragedy of the Commons', *Science*, Vol. 126 (1968) 1243-48

23 PERRINS, CHRISTOPHER. 'Survival of Young Swifts in Relation to Brood Size'. *Nature*, Vol. 201 (1964) 1147-48

24 LACK, DAVID. *Population Studies of Birds* (London, Oxford University Press 1966)

25 BRIERLEY, J. K. *Biology and the Social Crisis* (London, Heinemann Educational Books 1967)

26 DEEVEY, EDWARD S. 'The Human Population', in: Garrett Hardin (ed.) *39 Steps to Biology* (Reading, W. H. Freeman 1968)

27 BIRDSELL, JOSEPH B. 'Some Environmental and Cultural Factors influencing the Structure of Australian Aboriginal Populations', *American Naturalist*, Vol. 87 (1953) 171-207

28 HAWLEY, A. H. *Quoted by* WEINER, J. S. 'Human Ecology', in: G. A. Harrison, J. S. Weiner, J. M. Tanner and N. A. Barnicot. *Human Biology* (Oxford University Press 1964)

29 WEINER, J. S. 'Human Ecology', in: G. A. Harrison, J. S. Weiner, J. M. Tanner and N. A. Barnicot. *Human Biology* (Oxford University Press 1964)

30 CLARK, F. LE GROS. Quoted by WEINER, J. S. 'Human Ecology', in G. A. Harrison, J. S. Weiner, J. M. Tanner and N. A. Barnicot. *Human Biology* (London, Oxford University Press 1964)

31 HARDIN, GARRETT. 'The Ancient and Honorable History of Contraception', in: Garrett Hardin (ed.) *Population, Evolution and Birth Control* (Reading, W. H. Freeman 1969)

32 WYNDHAM, JOHN. *The Seeds of Time* (London, Michael Joseph 1956)

33 VON KOENIGSWALD, G. H. R. *Meeting Prehistoric Man* (London, Thames & Hudson 1956)

34 MONTAGU, M. F. ASHLEY. *Man in Process* (London, Mentor Books 1961)

35 BRIERLEY, JOHN. *A Natural History of Man* (London, Heinemann Educational Books 1970)

36 LANGER, WILLIAM L. 'The Black Death', in: Garrett Hardin (ed.) *39 Steps to Biology* (Reading, W. H. Freeman 1968)

37 LONGMATE, NORMAN. *King Cholera* (London, Hamish Hamilton 1966)

38 ZINSSER, HANS. *Rats, Lice and History* (London, Bantam Classics 1960)

39 LANGER, WILLIAM L. 'Checks on Population Growth: 1750-1850', *Scientific American*, Vol. 226 (1972) 92-9

40 EHRLICH, PAUL R. and EHRLICH, ANNE H. *Population, Resources, Environment* (Reading, W. H. Freeman 1972)

41 WYNNE-EDWARDS, V. C. 'Population Control in Animals', in Garrett Hardin (ed.), *39 Steps to Biology* (Reading, W. H. Freeman 1968)

3 The Magic of the Group

'All are but parts of one stupendous whole,
whose body Nature is.'

Pope: *Essay on Man*

Arthur Koestler[1] writes: 'The attempt to reduce the complex behaviour of man to the hypothetical "atoms of behaviour" found in lower mammals produced next to nothing that is relevant'. He is reacting to some of the tenets of what he thinks is modern psychology, particularly the 'monumental superstition' (his phrase) of Behaviourism; and I would be the first to agree with what he says. All he is really doing is firing another shot in a long and bitter campaign whose battle lines were already clearly apparent to Aristotle and Democritus. The crux of the argument lies in the question: What is life? To one side of the argument, best simply called *mechanism*, the answer is: Life is merely matter arranged in a particular way; the difference between living and non-living resides solely in their arrangement of the particles of matter. But the advocate for the other side (*vitalism*) says: Life consists of two separate factors – (*i*) matter, and (*ii*) a life principle which is immaterial but which shapes and organizes the matter; non-living consists of matter only.[2]

This distinction is not as academic as it sounds, for it has an immediate consequence in one's practical approach to the study of life. If the mechanist is right then life is reducible to a series of physical and chemical reactions; and all one has to do is to sort them out, lay them in a neat row on the dissecting table (or one of its more complicated equivalents, such as an electron microscope) and there you are: you know what life is. Behaviourism is basically a form of psychological mechanism, but the tendency towards mechanism (or atomism, or reductionism) occurs throughout the biological sciences. One of its most spectacular successes has been in what is called *molecular biology*; in G. G. Simpson's (1962[3]) apt phrasing: 'The gaudiest bandwagon [in biology] just now is manned by reductionists, is travelling on biochemical and biophysical roads, and carries a banner with a strange device: DNA'. I have never read a popular account of research on DNA, RNA, and all the rest of it which has not solemnly assured me that the work is basically concerned with the *secret of life* (also called the code of life or the language of the genes). A recent instance is afforded by a newspaper review[4] of Jacques Monod's super-mechanistic *Chance and Necessity*:[5] 'The real, inner secret of life', the reviewer informs me, 'was explained by Watson and Crick . . . When scientists know so much about life it seems that only the details remain to be filled in.'

To the vitalist, of course, all this just won't do. If there really is a vital factor over and above the mere particles of matter such as DNA, then chemical and physical analyses are futile: you cannot trap a ghost. But even when the vitalist eventually admitted that basically he was calling on the supernatural to explain life (which isn't allowed by the rules of the game), his place was quickly taken by the *holist* or compositionist (in psychology: the *gestalt* psychologist). The concept of holism is simply that *the whole is greater than the sum of its parts*: there are not only independent elements and one-way reactions, but also interrelations, complex sequences which influence one another mutually, feedback loops and all the rest of it. Arthur Koestler[1] has an apt analogy: if you wanted to find out what makes up a cathedral, chemical analysis of the bricks and mortar of which it is built would tell you rather little. A cathedral consists of bricks *plus*

mortar *plus* an enormously intricate set of spatial relationships between them. Or to quote Simpson[6] again: 'One way
to analyse the living system is to take it apart, but then its
characteristics *as a system* are lost, and those are the irre-
ducible features of life'.

It is fair to say that the holistic approach is slowly gaining
the upper hand in biology today. As Garrett Hardin[7] points
out: 'the great emphasis on molecular biology in biology
curricula is . . . out of phase with historical realities . . .
Already molecular biology shows signs of aging, if not senil-
ity'. And once more we must let Simpson have the last
word:[6]

> 'Nothing that has so far been learned about DNA has
> helped significantly to understand the nature of man or of
> any other whole organism . . . We really do not know why
> or how the specification of a particular congeries of DNA
> molecules and a specific set of corresponding proteins pro-
> duce in one case a rosebush and in another case a man.
> That is the "secret of life" and the "language of the gene",
> and DNA in itself is obviously not the answer.'

But in any case we can conclude that holism is getting to
be all the rage in biology today. It therefore becomes increasingly pertinent to ask: Just what is this *whole* that we
are trying to study? What is the fundamental unit of life, and
ipso facto of organic evolution?

Wynne-Edwards[8] obviously has an answer at his finger-
tips: it is the population. His prudent individual restrains its
selfish drives for the good of the *population as a whole*.
Lorenz,[9] too, has resolved the problem to his own satisfaction
when he writes: 'When . . . a species of animals develops a
weapon which may destroy a fellow-member . . . then . . . it
must develop a social inhibition to prevent a usage [of the
weapon] which could endanger the existence of the species'.

Lorenz's answer is the *species*. If you seek an answer in any of the modern great books of evolution (such as the voluminous works of Theodosius Dobzhansky and Ernest Mayr[10]) you will not find one very definitely stated, but the general impression you will get will be that the population is the critical unit for our purposes. And I recall reading a paper in a recent issue of *The American Zoologist* which assured me that the fundamental unit upon which natural selection works is the *ecosystem*: the whole interrelated system of the living organisms and their environment in any given area.

In a variation of an old conundrum: Suppose you were an evolutionary biologist about to be cast away on a desert island, and you were allowed to take only two evolutionary books with you. Which two would you take? Before 1966 that would have been a puzzle indeed, but it is no longer. For in that year George C. Williams' *Adaptation and Natural Selection*[11] was published, and it is the most important book on evolution since *On the Origin of Species*. If you had any sense those are the two books you would tuck firmly in your life-jacket as you leapt for the rail.

Williams' book isn't what an evolutionary textbook should be. It has no photographs, barely any diagrams, no complicated tables, not all that many references. It is difficult reading. And all it really does is to remind us of something that we knew all along: natural selection is differential reproduction among genotypes. Every biologist accepts that; it is almost self-evident. But what Williams does is to force us to see the consequences of that fact; and it suddenly dawns on us that a huge proportion of what has been written about evolution is, in effect, vacuous. It is as if a passer-by were to shout up to an engineer finishing the thirtieth storey of his skyscraper (and finishing it very beautifully, too, with all sorts of elegant little decorations and refinements) that he had forgotten to put in any foundations, and that the whole edifice was beginning to crumble. The building is a substantial part of modern evolutionary dogma, and the passer-by is George C. Williams.

Biology is suffering from rampant holism. There is a certain magic about wholeness . . . the whole is greater than the sum of its parts. There is a fine, mystical ring about that, particularly since, arithmetically speaking, the one thing a whole *cannot* be is something greater than the sum of its parts. There is the Walt Disney-inspired reverence towards Nature's Half Acre, where each organism has a job to do, and the individual actions of all of them result in a stable, integrated whole where Mother Nature looks after her own. There is awe and reverence when we look at an ant colony; each individual by itself is nothing, but all work together to achieve a unitary and viable system. There are Wynne-Edwards' and Ardrey's splendid visions of populations which act as concerted units for their own good, and Lorenz's weapon-carrying individuals who inhibit their destructive potential for the good of the whole species to which they belong. And there is the modern worship of the ecosystem as a functioning entity whose parts are all interrelated to form a super-whole . . . pick a flower and a polar bear trembles. And yet it is all 'a tale told by an idiot, full of sound and fury, signifying nothing'.

Natural selection is differential reproduction among genotypes. We already know what that means, from Chapter 2 (page 30). The genotype is the genetic constitution of an individual organism; each genotype (except in the cases of monozygotic twins and clones) is unique. According to the particular make-up of its genotype an organism will be more or less fit in a given environment: it will leave more or fewer offspring. The genes of those individuals who leave the most offspring will be represented in proportionally greater amounts in the next generation; the genetic constitution of

the population will have changed; evolution will have occurred.

We may seem to be labouring the point; the important
thing about all this is that it is clearly the *individual* who is
the unit of selection. Natural selection has only one criterion
to go on: the number of offspring left by each individual.
Obviously, therefore, the individuals who prosper are those
who maximize their own reproduction, without regard to
what effect this may have on anybody else. No other sort of
individual could survive in the system.

Where does this lead us? It brings us to the conclusion
that every organism – mollusc, marlin, muscovy, mouse or
man – must be basically selfish. What selection judges it by
is how well it perpetuates its own self-interest; what it must
do is to perpetuate it as successfully as possible. It should
show no compunction for anyone else; more than that, if
treading on other peoples' toes advances its cause, then it
should actively seek to be a toe-treader. It can at no time
afford to divert to anyone else the minutest amount of energy
which it could expend on itself. Selfishness must be the order
of the day and altruism must be recognized as the grossest of
foolishness.

There is, of course, one concession that must be made in
this argument. While it is true, as we have said, that each
total genotype is unique, it is also true that related individuals
have a substantial proportion of their genotype in common.
Thus the unit of selection, the whole that we are interested
in, is not really the single individual. It is that individual and
his kin: his mate, his offspring, his siblings, his parents (and,
to a lesser extent, his nieces, nephews, cousins, uncles and
so on). For they are not like the rest of the population: they
share a high proportion of their genes with him. Parents and
children have on average half their genes in common, as do
brothers and sisters. Grandparents and grandchildren have

one quarter in common; so do first cousins. The real unit that we are looking for is *the individual and his genetic lineage*. Selection really operates between lineages, favouring those lineages characterized by the best reproductive performance. Thus a mother who sacrifices her life for her offspring is ensuring that her genes are perpetuated in them; but no mother should be prepared to sacrifice her life – or indeed, expend any energy at all – for a completely unrelated individual. The benefits bestowed on any individual should be in proportion to the closeness of your relationship with it: you may sacrifice your life for your son; you would hardly do it for your fifth cousin three times removed. But you might lend your cousin five pounds, something you would not do for a perfect stranger.

All this leads to one conclusion: that holistic interpretations in biology must stop at the individual and his lineage – these together constitute the whole that is 'greater' than the sum of its parts. *They* are the units of selection; not populations, not species. Every biological phenomenon that we see must be explicable in just these terms; if you can't do it in these terms then you've misinterpreted the phenomenon: have another look at it.

What of Lorenz's kind-hearted predator which doesn't use its weapons on conspecifics? If what I am saying is right the animal should use its weapons, should eliminate its non-kin fellows, because they are competitors for food and other resources. The most efficient way of ensuring the maximum supply of resources for yourself *would* be to kill all your competitors. So why doesn't it happen?

The answer is twofold. First, of course, it *does* happen. There are plenty of records of animals of the same species killing each other. But second, let's ask another question: How easy is it for two unarmed, evenly-matched animals to kill each other? (By unarmed we mean unarmed with manufactured weapons, of course.) Very difficult, obviously. The human sport of boxing bears witness: the reason it is a sport is that we know that the chance of one unarmed man killing another is infinitesimally small, even though the idea of the 'game' is for the men to hit each other as hard as they possibly can, and inflict as much short-term damage as they are able. On the other hand boxers do get damaged to a greater or lesser extent while pursuing their profession, and the longer they go on the more damage they suffer. The point is that a canary, or a stag, or a lion, or what you will, in attempting to kill a conspecific, runs an exceedingly high chance that it will itself be injured in the process. John Maynard Smith's recent analysis[12] of animal conflict in terms of games theory shows that an animal which adopts a 're-taliator' strategy (use dangerous tactics only when provoked) is far fitter than one which employs a 'hawk' strategy (always use dangerous tactics). It is better by far to bluff and bluster for as long as possible; to engage in mortal combat is the very last resort. You may win, but in doing so it is almost certain that you will lose an eye, or puncture a lung, or break a bone; and what a nasty blot that would be on your nice clean fitness sheet. Your compatriot who pushes his luck as far as he can, but if all else fails gives in gracefully, is doing a much better job of enhancing his fitness than such hyper-aggressive pugilists as yourself.

That seems to me to be an eminently reasonable explanation. Bearing in mind the mode of operation of natural selection, we know that Lorenz's benefit-to-the-species explanation had to be wrong, and that we had to find an alternative, benefit-to-the-individual one. And it wasn't really very hard to find. Likewise, we found one quite easily when dealing with Wynne-Edwards' prudential restraint. His was a good-of-the-population explanation; we knew, therefore, that something was wrong with it. And we found that the only reason that an individual may appear to be restraining its reproductive rate is that clutch or litter size is dictated by the number of young that can be raised, not merely the number that can be born.

But . . . what's wrong with this? Let's suppose we have two populations. In one of them every single individual shows prudential restraint and adjusts its reproductive rate to prevailing conditions. In the other everyone just reproduces like hell regardless. A famine strikes. What happens? The population with restraint will cut down on procreation, resulting in fewer mouths to feed, in turn resulting in survival of a substantial proportion of the population. The one without restraint breeds itself into oblivion; starves itself into extinction. Population A survives; Population B does not. Why couldn't natural selection act in this way, selecting not between individuals but between *groups*?

That is the theory of group selection, and it is also Wynne-Edwards' answer to his critics. It's a nice idea: commonsensical, appealing, straightforward. But let's have a closer look at it.

For the theory to work, Population A must be composed entirely and exclusively of individuals who show restraint; if just one unrestrained individual were present he would outbreed everyone else and his genetic constitution would eventually come to characterize the whole population. But how are we going to fix the genotype for prudential restraint in a whole population? It clearly cannot be fixed by ordinary natural selection: such selection will in fact act against it, bcause its bearers leave fewer progeny than everyone else. The only way it could be fixed, if you work it out, is by pure luck, or, in the jargon, 'genetic drift': purely random or accidental events. It just could happen, for example. that you got a new population founded by only three or four individuals, all of whom, by sheer chance, showed prudential restraint: that would be genetic drift. Well and good. But merely founding the thing isn't enough – you've got to maintain it. You can't afford to have even one immigrant who isn't a prudential restrainer. You mustn't have even one mutation: restraint to non-restraint. The moment either of those things happens your nice little restrained population has had it; *individual* selection will see to that.

It can in fact be shown that a species in which random processes such as genetic drift are going to be important must have a certain rigidly defined population structure. It must be split into a number of sub-populations, each of a certain size, with a certain amount of isolation between them, and so on. No one has ever found an animal population with quite this structure: it follows that genetic drift in this context is strictly in the realms of cloud-cuckoo biology. And no genetic drift: no prudential restraint. It's as simple as that. When Robert Ardrey[13] writes: 'To the discomfort of more conservative biologists, Wynne-Edwards proposed group selection . . .', he has made a *lapsus calami* or two. For *discomfort* he should have written *incredulity*; and for *conservative, knowledgeable*. When he writes: 'Wynne-Edwards' group selection . . . provides a genetic explanation for the self-regulation of animal numbers', we can probably let that pass. A non-explanation is presumably quite in order for a non-event. And perhaps we can include one more quote, from a review by the ornithologist Dean Amadon[14] of *Animal Dispersion in Relation to Social Behaviour*. After acknowledging that Wynne-Edwards has produced an interesting descriptive compendium of animal behaviour, he concludes: '. . . the reviewer admits some mystification. So far as he can see, no genetic model for such group selection is here proposed'.

But what G. C. Williams tell us in *Adaptation and Natural Selection* is that the *modus operandi* of natural selection has consequences that reach much further than just one man's ideas about aggression, or another's theories of population control. He is making the point that *any* phenomenon, *any* effect, which appears to be a group or population function, can in fact only be a summation of individual functions. The whole, when it is a whole population or a whole species, is simply and only the sum of its parts. Biology has been busily describing group functions left, right and centre, but all they are is summations of individual functions.

Let's take a simple example: birds are superbly adapted for flying. What do we understand by that statement? Does it mean that bird-dom, as a whole, has been shaped by selection in such a way that it is characterized by flight? Not at all. It means that in the past there were birds which flew rather badly and others that flew very well; because of the enormous advantage it conferred on them, the good flyers out-reproduced the poor ones. In time, therefore, most lineages of birds became good flyers, as a result of the individual adaptation of each lineage. The fact that all birds today are good flyers is a simple arithmetic summation of the adaptedness of all these lineages.

In this case, of course, the argument is academic, even trivial; but in others it is of enormous significance. If every group phenomenon must be explicable in individual terms we have to do some drastic restructuring of our concept of the biological world.

What, for instance, is a society? Wynne-Edwards (enthusiastically endorsed by Ardrey) says it is 'a group of individuals competing for conventional prizes by conventional methods'. The analogy is to conventions between nations, to limit nuclear weapons, for example, or the exploitation of certain resources such as fisheries. The animals, too, have conventions: don't breed if food is short; don't kill conspecifics; respect other peoples' territories; and so on. The prizes are also conventional: you don't actually kill your competitor, for instance (which would be a real prize); by means of a conventional display you merely show him who's the boss. Another, and very common, way of looking at animal societies is to interpret them as groups of individuals which ignore their own good and work together for the good of the group. This is the way in which W. C. Allee[15] regards a flock of hens, for instance: it has a 'peck order' to reduce stress and fighting; each hen learns her place and subjugates her individual motivations for the benefit of the flock as a whole.

It is clear that none of this is acceptable. If we want to define a society we can do it only from the viewpoint of the individual, and our definition would have to be something like: A society is a group of individuals in which each co-operates with the others only to the extent that its own fitness is thereby enhanced. Obviously in complex societies such as those of man and other primates there will be a welter of overlapping interests, and determining the adaptive significance of each particular social act will often be difficult. But the general rule will always be: look after yourself and your kin first, but if doing this efficiently requires co-operation with non-kin, then by all means co-operate. Of course co-operation will be limited to your own social group, because it includes the individuals most likely to be of assistance to you. In a strictly limited sense the unit of selection then becomes a small group of lineages rather than a single one; but this is still an entirely different kettle of fish from a whole population or species.

Men are social; men are also selfish. There can be little doubt that they evolved in a context of small and mutually hostile tribes, and each member co-operated with the rest of the tribe (or group) in so far as it facilitated his own reproductive success. How true is this of man today?

There are two problems to be overcome in getting to grips with this question. One is the extreme reluctance of man to see himself as a selfish, non-altruistic creature, as R. D. Alexander[16] has pointed out. What about the man who jumps into the sea to save a drowning (and unrelated) child? Surely that's an altruistic thing to do! And what about the public benefactor who gives huge sums to charity? And the soldier who falls on a grenade to save his comrades? And the German officer who followed Hitler about with a time-bomb in each pocket, in an attempt to blow Hitler (and, willy-nilly, himself) into oblivion? And the Japanese kamikaze pilots? And . . . and . . . and . . .?

Yes, I'm aware of all that. Just one comment which is relevant at this stage; we'll come across more points later. But let's note for now, again with Alexander, that any urban, national or world problem is at the same time a *personal* problem. What may appear to be an act of supreme self-sacrifice for the public good may in fact be motivated by the threat as it applies to one's own lineage (and quite incidentally to the rest of the country). Do men go to war because they want to honour their country's glorious name, or because they are worried about the threat that the enemy represents to them, to their wives, children, homes, way of life? When a conservationist marches in protest at the destruction of a natural asset is he angered because future generations will be deprived of it? Or is it because *he* and his children and grandchildren (along with all those irrelevant everybody-elses) will miss out?

This is the second problem: the modern individual does not belong to just one tribe; he belongs to many, simultaneously. I belong to my family group, but also to a university community. Within the university I belong to a faculty; within the faculty to a department; within the department to a research group. At different times I identify with all these groupings: I ally myself with fellow-members of the science faculty 'against' the arts faculty: with fellow biologists against physical scientists; with fellow zoologists against botanists; with fellow holistic zoologists against atomistic zoologists. I am switching and modifying allegiances all the time, according to conditions. It is no longer as simple as the old situation of a tribal in-group, to whose members one showed altruism; and a foreigner out-group, to whose members one showed hostility. For as well as all these other group allegiances I am also a Melbournian, a Victorian, and an Australian; the in-group to which I belong gets progressively bigger. If Australia were under dire threat of attack by another nation most of the minor groupings would become insignificant. The greater the threat, the bigger the group that the individual will identify with, which is of course a very adaptive way for him to behave.

Thus the line separating those-whom-I-co-operate-with from those-whom-I-don't-co-operate-with is, in man, a highly mobile one. Normally my neighbour and I treat each other with indifference, but if the council decides to spray our gardens with dieldrin (to 'eradicate' Argentine ants) we become a co-operating unit against the common threat. The point is that, no matter what the situation, the individual's co-operation or non-co-operation is based on which will contribute more to his own well-being. His motive is always selfish: he will co-operate, even be apparently altruistic, *if it does him good*; and for no other reason.

All this has repercussions on a variety of issues. Take pollution, for instance: what about a brewery which insists on selling its beer in those non-biodegradable and generally almost indestructible aluminium cans? All the brewery is interested in is selling more beer, i.e. doing itself some good. The fact that the cans litter the countryside is just not relevant. Until, of course, there is an outcry about ecology and pollution and so on, when the brewery suddenly starts recycling (or, more likely, makes a token gesture towards recycling) its cans. You may say that they are acting *pro bono publico*, and where does that leave the selfishness hypothesis? But in fact the brewery has merely decided that there are enough people kicking up a fuss about aluminium cans to affect sales; it will therefore be to its own good if it pretends to be doing something about it. And the louder it pretends the more effective it will be; with any luck it will make the pollution issue into a real selling point. This does not imply any criticism of the brewery; I am merely pointing out that, because breweries are run by human beings, it is inevitable that they should behave in this manner. Any other behaviour would be non-adaptive; damned stupid, in fact. And you can apply this argument to anything you please: motor cars, mining, smog, water pollution and all the rest of it.

There is always a self-centred reason for apparently altruistic acts. Here's one hypothesis about the soldier who falls on the grenade (Alexander has another). This soldier is unpopular, friendless, not really one of the boys. If he *does* fall on the grenade there is just a chance that he will survive; and of course if he survives he will be everybody's mate, a hero, a superboy. If he doesn't fall on it there is absolutely no chance that he will undergo this transformation.

What if you jump into the sea to save a drowning child? If you are a competent swimmer the chance that you will survive is excellent; and regardless of whether you save the child or not you will have done yourself a power of good in the public eye. You are in fact conferring a considerable benefit on yourself at a very low cost.

But (you may well protest) when you see a drowning child you don't think: Hmmm . . . what are the chances of my saving this kid and earning some kudos . . . hmmm . . . yes, it's worth a try. Of course you don't. But your lineage has been experiencing selective pressure for *x* thousand generations to act in an appropriate manner in countless situations like this. It's not a matter of conscious decision. Those who acted rashly were weeded out: we are the descendants of those who acted wisely.

On the other hand the mention of children does bring up an interesting point. We tend to be very discriminating with regard to adults, but a child – any child – is likely to elicit compassion and affection from us. We react to the *generalized* features of young humans: smallness, roundness, helplessness. This is why organizations such as famine relief groups almost always use photographs of starving children in their propaganda: they know that these are most effective in attracting care and sympathy. So this is one case where our adaptive selfishness is reduced somewhat, and it stems of course from the fact that for most of our evolutionary history the only children we met were our own or those of kin or other group members. The safest policy, evolutionary-fitness-wise, was therefore to react positively to *any* child.

Actually it has overflowed a little beyond this. Affection is released in us by virtually any young animal – puppy, kitten, bear cub, chick – as long as it has the generalized infantile features of roundness, softness, warmth, 'cuddliness'. You have only to look at Figure 277 in Eibl-Eibesfeldt's *Ethology: The Biology of Behaviour*[17] to see what I mean. Thus, as J. M. Smith[18] puts it, 'the protective responses shown by female mammals to the young of their own and often of other species probably evolved because the most efficient way of ensuring that a female will protect her own young is that she should evolve an instinctive response to certain very generalized features of young mammals. Such undiscriminating responses can lay a species open to exploitation by others; for example, many birds are exploited by cuckoos, ants are exploited by numerous species of insects, and women are exploited by lapdogs'.

But it is still a perfectly valid general rule that each individual is governed first and foremost by self-interest; and secondly by the interests of his group as they affect him. The cases Smith discusses are really examples of selfishness misfiring, of energy accidentally being expended on a stranger. And it is the very nature of adaptive selfishness – the attempt to bestow care only on members of one's own lineage – that is the weakness in the system. In trying to make assurance doubly sure that care *is* given to anyone likely to be kin, it is sometimes fortuitously given to someone who is not.

None of this alters the general thesis: if there are conventions, it is because they are doing someone some good. If a group refrains from fighting, or destroying, or polluting, or whatever, it is purely and simply because it *pays* to refrain. The belief that is widely held, that an individual who 'intends only his own gain' is 'led by an invisible hand to promote . . . the public interest' (Adam Smith, 1776, quoted by Garrett Hardin[19]) is not defensible in any manner that I can see. Consequently any practice, any system of *mores*, any philosophy, that is based on the 'private interest=public good' idea is a false god. It has always been, will always be, can only be, the case that each individual strives to obtain as large as possible a share of resources for himself and his lineage; and to do this he often finds it useful to co-operate with some other individuals, i.e. join a group, so that he can compete more effectively with still other individuals and groups.

I have on my shelves a book called *From Magic to Science*; it is a history of medicine. While I doubt the implication that modern medicine has entirely divested itself of its magical past, the title does illustrate what has happened to the concept of the group. There is no magic in groups: they are simply summations of individuals; their behaviour the summation of individual behaviour. There is no 'something else', no vital factor or group principle involved; if a group appears to show certain attributes it is only because the individuals composing it show those attributes. A group is not guided or governed by any superior influence; it simply drifts with the tides generated by its competent individuals.

One more apparent exception, and one more general principle, and then we shall be done with groups for the moment. Various investigators of laboratory rodent populations, such as John Calhoun[20] with rats and Peter Crowcroft[21] with mice, have produced results which seem to give the lie to the selfishness hypothesis. If you provide a caged colony of rats or mice with excess food and then stand back and watch, you find, not surprisingly, that the colony grows. But after a while strange things begin to happen. In one of Crowcroft's experiments, when a certain level of crowding was reached, the vast majority of females simply ceased to function sexually: they never came into oestrus. The population stopped growing; the curve levelled out. Calhoun's rats in similar circumstances also began to behave in extraordinary ways; males became super-aggressive or super-passive or homosexual or cannibalistic; females ceased to care for their young and infant mortality skyrocketed. Again, the population stopped growing.

Interpretation One: the individuals realized that they were overcrowded and stopped reproducing so as not to overtax their living space and resources (i.e. the individuals sacrificed their own selfish reproductive drive for the good of the colony as a whole). Implication One: if and when man gets overcrowded he'll simply stop reproducing and everything will be OK.

Interpretation Two: the cessation of normal reproductive activity does not *prevent* overcrowding; it comes into play only *after* overcrowding is already established. It is in fact a pathological manifestation of crowding stress; failure to reproduce is an effect, not a function, of crowding. Implication Two: all this has no relevance whatsoever to man. Long before he reaches a pathological level of crowding he will have run out of food or raw materials or both. Since people living in New York and Tokyo and Calcutta show no particular reluctance to breed it is clear that their levels of crowding, high as they are, do not result in any significant reproductive stress. We can take cold comfort in the assurance that, whatever it is that gets us in the end, it certainly won't be crowding stress.

One final word: what about survival of the species? How many times have you read that such-and-such is adaptive because it results in survival of the species? Mother Nature, for instance, knows that fish fry suffer enormous mortality; to compensate for this she endows fish with such gigantic reproductive capabilities that at least a few fry will always make it and the species will survive. Again, Mother Nature knows that too many caterpillars would defoliate whole forests and starve themselves into extinction, so she thoughtfully provides a whole host of predators and parasites of caterpillars; they keep the system in balance and ensure both that the forest survives and that a few caterpillars get to be butterflies and perpetuate the species.

Mother Nature, in fact, doesn't give a damn about survival of the species. Species are groups, just like any other groups, and selection doesn't operate at the group level. That each individual is concerned with looking after only its own lineage can be demonstrated by a hundred-and-one examples. A penguin returning from a fishing trip to the nursery, where her progeny stand among thousands of their fellows (and to us, at least, they all look exactly the same), ignores all youngsters but her own, and regurgitates fish for them alone. If she had survival of the species in mind she ought to feed any or all of them. A wandering herring gull chick faces the certainty of being ejected from all nests but its own, and the distinct possibility of being killed or injured if it stops in a strange nest. If the owners of the strange nest were motivated by thoughts of species survival, they ought to . . . etc., etc. A seal pup galumphing up the beach is firmly prevented from suckling by all cows but its mother. If . . . and so on.

Survival of the species is merely the survival of a number of individual lineages, all summed together. If the individuals of a species are behaving in a way which promotes their survival then, willy-nilly, the species survives, as a simple arithmetic consequence. If enough individuals behave in ways which militate against their survival then, again as a statistical consequence, the species is extinguished. That's the way it is: drongos or dinosaurs, horses or humming-birds, microbes or men; it makes not the least difference. There is no invisible hand promoting species survival; natural selection has never, nor can it ever, act in the interests of species *per se*. In the case of *Homo sapiens*, of course, natural selection is favouring those who are doing the good old things in the most efficient way possible; procreating, exploiting resources, resisting environmental stresses. And the summation of all these hundreds of millions of individual strivings for survival is the very last thing that is likely to result in survival of the species.

NOTES

1 KOESTLER, ARTHUR. *The Ghost in the Machine* (London, Hutchinson 1967)
2 SCHUBERT-SOLDERN, R. *Mechanism and Vitalism* (London, Burns and Oates 1962)
3 SIMPSON, GEORGE GAYLORD. 'The Status of the Study of Organisms', *American Scientist*, Vol. 50 (1962) 36-45
4 THE AGE, MELBOURNE, 8 April 1972
5 MONOD, JACQUES. *Chance and Necessity* (London, Collins 1972)

L.G.

6 SIMPSON, GEORGE GAYLORD. *Biology and Man* (New York, Harcourt, Brace and World 1969)

7 HARDIN, GARRETT. 'A Path to Relevant Teaching', *Bio-Science*, Vol. 20 (1970) 488-90

8 WYNNE-EDWARDS, V. C. *Animal Dispersion in Relation to Social Behaviour* (Edinburgh, Oliver and Boyd 1962)

9 LORENZ, KONRAD. *King Solomon's Ring* (London, Methuen 1952)

10 For example: DOBZHANSKY, THEODOSIUS. *Genetics of the Evolutionary Process* (Columbia University Press 1970) MAYR, ERNST. *Populations, Species and Evolution* (The Belknap Press of Harvard University Press 1970)

11 WILLIAMS, GEORGE C. *Adaptation and Natural Selection* (Princeton University Press 1966)

12 SMITH, J. M. and PRICE, G. R. 'The Logic of Animal Conflict', *Nature*, Vol. 246 (1973) 15-18

13 ARDREY, ROBERT. *The Social Contract* (London, Collins 1970)

14 AMADON, DEAN. 'Population Control in Nature', *Evolution*, Vol. 16 (1962) 530

15 ALLEE, W. C. *Co-operation Among Animals* (London, Pitman and Sons 1951)

16 ALEXANDER, R. D. 'The Search for an Evolutionary Philosophy of Man', *Proceedings of the Royal Society of Victoria*, Vol. 84 (1971) 99-120

17 EIBL-EIBESFELDT, I. *Ethology: The Biology of Behaviour* (New York, Holt, Rinehart and Winston 1970)

18 SMITH, JOHN MAYNARD. *The Theory of Evolution* (London, Penguin Books 1968)

19 HARDIN, GARRETT. 'The Tragedy of the Commons', *Science*, Vol. 162 (1968) 1243-48

20 CALHOUN, JOHN. 'Population Density and Social Pathology', in: Garrett Hardin (ed.), *39 Steps to Biology* (Reading, W. H. Freeman 1968)

21 CROWCROFT, PETER. *Mice All Over* (Henley-on-Thames, G. T. Foulis 1968)

4 The Pathological Progressive

'Progress is the law of life.'
Browning: Paracelsus

In a remote valley in New Guinea there lives a people called the Tsembaga. When the Michigan anthropologist Roy Rappaport[1] visited them in 1962-63, there were 204 of them, and their territory comprised 3.2 square miles, varying in altitude from 2,200 to 7,200 feet. Their population density was thus 64 persons to the square mile (that of the USA is 55 people per square mile).

The Tsembaga (apart, of course, from being ignorant and heathen savages) are practitioners of the art of 'swiddening', also called slash-and-burn agriculture. They cut clearings in the tropical rainforest, burn the cuttings, and plant and harvest gardens for one to three years. The clearing is then abandoned and allowed to revert to forest; meanwhile new clearings will have been made somewhere else. At any one time only 90-100 acres are under cultivation; about ninety per cent of the potentially arable land is therefore lying fallow.

A mature garden is an absolute shambles. Bananas, taros, yams, sweet potatoes, sugar cane, cassava, leafy greens, corn, cucumbers, asparagus, pumpkins; all are growing profusely over, under and among each other. The sweet potato leaves form a mat on the ground and everything else has to find its way through the mat. Worse, most of the tree stumps are left in place (they are used as stakes for tying up sugar cane, for example) and many of them start to regenerate; seeds also blow in from the neighbouring forest and seedling trees begin to sprout all over the show. Herbaceous weeds are removed but the tree seedlings are left; they are soon so big that working in the garden becomes forbiddingly laborious, and it is often abandoned even before it is completely harvested.

But the Tsembaga do not live by gardens alone; they are also swineherds. Much of the food grown in the gardens is fed to the pigs. When Rappaport was there the herd had reached a size of 169, and it was eating, among other things, half of the sweet potato crop and eighty-two per cent of the cassava crop. The pigs, in turn, are eaten by the Tsembaga, but only in very special circumstances. Every decade or so there is a festival when all the adult and many young pigs are killed and eaten; in this case the 169 pigs were reduced to 60 (in terms of live weight the herd had been reduced six-fold). The festival is one step in a cycle which later includes tribal warfare; apart from this, pigs arc rarely slaughtered except for rituals associated with sickness and death. Feral pigs are eaten whenever caught, and other sources of protein include mammals, birds, reptiles and insects caught in the forest.

The typical Tsembaga garden would be a nightmare to the backyard vegetable plot enthusiast; crops growing higgledy-piggledy all over each other; not a neat row in sight; trees coming up here, there and everywhere. It's just the sort of thing that you can imagine Michener's Abner Hale having a fit over. And how inefficient the whole thing is: instead of clearing the jungle properly they do it in this half-hearted manner and then abandon it to start all over again somewhere else. And what a way to husband livestock! – going virtually without meat for years on end and then having a meat orgy and cramming yourself with pork. It's like one of those 'What is Wrong with this Picture?' puzzles in a children's magazine where the dog is up a tree and the cat is burying a bone; it's a sort of compendium of absurd agriculture.

Australians also set out to farm their rainforests; only, being of good Western European stock, they did it properly. They got right down to business with the axe, the saw and the bulldozer, and when they made a clearing it stayed a clearing. Then they turned the land over to monoculture of dairy cattle, or maize, or sugar cane; no mucking about with messy, mixed-up gardens for them.

Perhaps we could take just one example, the Dorrigo Plateau in eastern New South Wales,[2] to demonstrate the spectacular results that these modern agricultural methods achieved. This was a stand of dense rainforest on red basaltic soil, and in 1909 an area of about 30,000 acres was thrown open for subdivision and put on the market for dairying and mixed farming. In 1917 the Dorrigo was being hailed as 'a splendid fertile district with an assured future', a place with 'great scope for industrious farms' where dairying had made 'wonderful progress'. A government propagandist wrote that there was room on the Dorrigo for 'thousands of industrious dairy farmers', due to the fact that it 'is one of the finest watered areas in Australia, if not the world'.

Forward to 1926 for another progress report on the Dorrigo settlement scheme: 'it is almost a complete failure, there being only 135 left out of the 160 who took up blocks, and these are . . . making a living . . . by labouring in timber and other industries. Not more than eight of the settlers are using the land for dairying or farming. The Surveyor who recommended [the Dorrigo] for settlement ought to be sacked'.

What went wrong? A 1943 report on the scheme has something to say on the subject: 'almost without exception all the farms have proved failures and incapable of supporting their owners . . . this on account of the nature of the soil, the upper horizon of which, being shallow, deteriorated early and soon eroded after being exposed'. It is now generally recognized that rainforest soils are of extremely limited fertility – the topsoil is often only a few inches in depth – and wholesale clearing leads inevitably to wholesale loss of fertility by leaching and erosion.

Let's have another look at the Tsembaga way of doing things. When a clearing is cut, the litter is burned on the spot, thereby releasing nutrients tied up in the trees to the soil. The crops, when they are planted, are intermingled in complex fashion (just as plant species in a rainforest are); some are deep and some shallow rooted; some are tall and some short (promoting photosynthetic efficiency); there are no vast monocultures, thus plant-specific pests are discouraged. The young trees which are left have the deepest roots of all and can assimilate nutrients which would otherwise be leached out, and the dense, varied mat of vegetation protects the soil from the onslaught of tropical downpours. The rapid re-growth of trees means that the clearings are abandoned before there is any serious depletion of nutrients, and it also results in quick regeneration of the forest, leaving the soil unprotected for the shortest possible time.

There appears to be a smattering of method in the Tsembaga madness, and even the pigs have their part to play. They are penned in abandoned gardens, where, as well as providing soil fertilizer, they complete the harvest by rooting out the remaining tubers, and facilitate forest re-growth by browsing on herbaceous weeds. They are also fed on domestic refuse, thus both food scraps and human excreta are effectively recycled and converted into high-quality protein.

But this is not the whole story of the Tsembaga. Rappaport carried out an analysis of the input to and yield from Tsembaga gardens in terms of energy: that is, for each calorie of work a Tsembaga gardener puts in, how many calories of food can he get out? The energy-consuming inputs include clearing, burning, fencing, weeding, harvesting and cartage of the produce after harvest. When the energy content of the harvest is balanced against all this it turns out that the labour-to-harvest ratio is of the order of 1 to 16, and may rise as high as 1 to 20. For every calorie consumed in toil, 16-20 calories are harvested as food. The energy economics of pig husbandry are, however, much worse. There the ratio varies from 1 to 2 down to 1 to a fraction. In this case the Tsembaga gardener is doing only marginally better than the modern mechanized farmer, who, considering the energy burned by his tractor, and also that consumed in producing fertilizers, pesticides, irrigation systems, etc., is putting in far more energy than he will ever get out as food.

What, then, is the fundamental difference between the Tsembaga super-garden and the Dorrigo disaster? In a word: technology. The Tsembaga must rely entirely on local biological processes for their energy; nothing else is available to them. The family which attempts some mistaken horticultural practice which tends to degrade the soil very quickly learns by bitter experience. Let us say, for instance, that you decide to try total and permanent clearing of the rainforest, *à la* Dorrigo. If you have the energy resources (i.e. technology) to manufacture and distribute vast quantities of fertilizer you might just get away with it for a while. But without that extra energy you've had it; you're finished, then and there. The Dorrigo mentality is: 'Hell, we've got the means: the machinery, the fertilizers, the *technology* – let's use them.' The other possible question that one might ask at this stage – is this the best, the wisest, thing to do? – simply doesn't get a mention. It is now implicitly accepted that any technological innovation is 'good'.

This is of course a hangover from the time when any technological innovation was good; that is, it achieved some essential function with greater ease, precision or rapidity than had been possible before. Bad technology either couldn't exist because its badness was instantaneously apparent (the square wheel had a remarkably short career), or because it became apparent in a short space of time and was phased out (total clearing of rainforest, for example). Part of the bind we are in today is that (*a*) our technology is so complex that we simply have no idea whether it's good, bad or indifferent (we tend to assume, therefore, that it's good); and (*b*) whatever goes wrong, you can always use a little more technology to fix it, to put it 'right' again.

'We can, therefore we shall' is the cry of the age. We don't have to mess about with half-baked clearings and manual harvest, so we bloody well won't. We'll do the thing properly, and if it turns sour, well, there are plenty more rainforests and the government will subsidize me for a new bulldozer.

There's a very simple reason for all this: inventiveness has been man's path to glory. Selective advantage has always accrued to those individuals (and their fellows) who discovered better ways of doing things. Imagine the australopithecine who threw stones matched against an australopithecine who hadn't discovered that stones could be thrown. And the arrow with the poisoned tip against the arrow without. And the tribe who used fire against the tribe who hadn't learned how to use it. And the wheel, the plough, the loom, the domestication of animals . . . ingenuity and resourcefulness have always been at a premium, and the groups with the greatest measures of each have always triumphed. The only criterion by which an innovation had to be judged was: does it improve our lives?, and the groups which included the greatest number of inventive individuals outsurvived and outreproduced everyone else. Ingenuity and willingness to innovate – progressiveness – are built into us.

We have here a situation exactly parallel to the overpopulation problem. It has always been selectively advantageous to try to outreproduce everybody else – 'Never,' as R. D. Alexander[3] says, 'has it been advantageous to restrict one's reproduction'. And yet we now face the prospect that the freedom of each of us to reproduce is going to be the end of all of us. So it is with technological advance. Any improvement in technology has always been favoured because of the improvement in fitness it conferred on its discoverers. And it is still true that the individual technologist (who, of course, acts entirely selfishly) does himself a power of good by inventing anything that represents a forward step, even if it's a bomb that kills 200,000 instead of 100,000 people at a time. It has never been advantageous to refrain from technological advance. But today technological progress, like population growth, has become pathological, because whether or not a particular advance improves human life is no longer a factor in deciding whether we should adopt it. 'Reproduction is good', says selection, so we reproduce; 'Technological innovation is good', so we innovate.

There is also a second problem here, and that is that we have got a little too clever for ourselves. Our technology has become so diabolically complex that we can no longer be sure of predicting the outcomes of the processes we devise. Thus in April 1968 in Melbourne there commenced the construction of a splendid, soaring box-girder bridge across the Yarra River. On 15 October 1970 one span of the partly-built bridge collapsed and thundered down into the mud and water, taking with it the lives of thirty-five workmen. The horrified state of Victoria instituted a Royal Commission to inquire into the disaster; it delivered its report on 14 July 1971.[4] The Commissioners found that the basic reason for the collapse was twofold: inadequate supervision by the bridge designers, and highly dangerous construction procedures by some of the contractors. But some interesting things emerge from a study of the fine print later in the report.

Page 35: 'some aspects of the stress analysis [of box girders] remain so far unresolved.' Page 43: 'experts could not agree on the determination of the theoretical failure loads for the panels.' Page 43 again: 'Many problems, including some that affected the design of West Gate Bridge, have not yet been solved.' Page 62: 'the attitude of both [engineers] to this problem appears to be that it is just too hard to solve analytically, and that an intelligent guess based on "engineering judgement" is the preferred solution.' Page 63: 'the stress pattern in the joint is complex and no analysis can claim to be precise' and 'the complex nature of this joint evades accurate analysis'.

And so it goes on. It is abundantly clear that at least some of the people involved in building 'one of the world's major bridges' didn't know what the hell they were doing. It comes as something of a shock to the layman, conditioned as he is to hero-worship of 'the expert', to find that building a gigantic bridge costing millions of dollars has such a substantial proportion of trial and error in it. But in reality it is the kind of thing we should be getting used to, in a world of technology run amok. As our technological marvels grow bigger and bigger they also come to encompass more and more imponderables, and we are gradually becoming accustomed to the West Gate Bridge effect in much of the technology that surrounds us.

But we cannot plead ignorance in the face of every disaster that overtakes us. We cannot excuse ourselves with the cry, 'We just didn't know . . . the analysis was too complex.' All too often we know, in greater or lesser detail, the effects that our wizardry is going to have, and we press on regardless in spite of this knowledge. Progress is, always has been, good; innovation has made us what we are; those, wholly and solely, constitute the justification for many of our more ridiculous follies.

Let's look at a few examples. Irrigation is one of man's oldest and most widespread forms of engineering; we can date 'hydraulic civilizations' back to at least 4000 BC.[5] And irrigation of arid land is now of course being held up as one of the great white hopes for feeding a hungry world. But we also know perfectly well that irrigation often causes serious problems, particularly in the very areas where we need it most: the arid and semi-arid zones. Large-scale irrigation requires dams; dams have large surface areas; dams therefore increase evaporation. Irrigation also causes groundwater levels to rise, and groundwater is often highly saline. Both of these factors lead to 'salting', of both soil and water run-off from irrigation areas. The South Australian Department of Agriculture[6] estimates that the problem of saline irrigation water is costing the state $2 million a year; we could cite similar stories from California, from Pakistan, from here, there and everywhere.

But irrigation is technology and technology is good; we should therefore not be surprised that such a disaster as the Aswan High Dam has been perpetrated. Question: What will be the major effect of the Aswan Dam? Answer: It will reduce the amount of water available to Egypt. (Reasoning: Evaporation from the lake will exceed earlier evaporation from the river. The evaporated water will fall as rain, most of it not on Egypt.) Question: But surely there must be other effects? Answer: Certainly. It will lead to salinity problems. It will decrease the fertility of the Nile delta. It has already decreased nutrient run-off into the sea to an extent demonstrated by the fact that the average annual sardine catch in the Eastern Mediterranean before closure of the dam was 18,000 tons; after closure it dropped to 400.*

It has, on the other hand, resulted in an explosive increase in

* This will, however, be partially compensated for by the development of a freshwater fishery on Lake Nasser.

populations of blood-flukes, which have an aquatic stage in their life-cycle, and which cause the disease schistosomiasis (bilharzia) in man. And it has wasted a hell of a lot of money, because estimates of the life of the reservoir run to a hundred years or so; then it will be silted up. Question: But there must be some benefits? Answer: Of course there are. The thing will increase the amount of irrigated land, and therefore help to raise food production. It will, in fact, supply food for a number of people less than that added by Egypt's population growth during the time it has taken to build the dam. And it will generate electricity, which is a good thing because electricity is going to be needed to power, *inter alia*, factories to make fertilizer to fertilize the Nile flood plains.[7]

But there is one enormous benefit of the scheme which we are overlooking: it has demonstrated anew man's ability to dominate his environment, in this case the Nile River; and technological domination is good. It is of course significant that the dam has been built by an industrialized nation in and for an undeveloped one. The present-day domination of the world by men of Western European descent stems almost entirely from their technical inventiveness. We are on the up and up; they (the Tsembaga, the Bushman, the Australian Aborigine, the American Indian, Old Uncle Tom Cobley and all) are well on their way to cultural or biological extinction. Ambrose Bierce's[8] definition is as timely as ever: '*Aborigines, n.* Persons of little worth found cumbering the soil of a newly discovered country. They soon cease to cumber; they fertilize.'

Another case in point: the supersonic transport (SST). What will be the major effects of the SST? Clearly they will be (*i*) to be a bloody nuisance to the vast majority of people with whom they come into proximity; (*ii*) to further foul up an already leprous atmosphere; and (*iii*) to gobble up with gargantuan bites our dwindling reserves of petroleum. An insignificant additional factor, which, if we have any sense of proportion at all, is barely worth mentioning, is that the SST will transport a minute number of people at an unnecessarily high speed. Of course we have again overlooked the most important function: the European SST will make a lot of money for some people in England and France. And they have a perfectly valid argument for the whole ludicrous exercise: it's *progress*. If it's better to go at 600 than at 300 m.p.h., then, obviously, 1,200 m.p.h. must be better still. The Americans for once are playing it cool: if the *Concorde* is a success then we can look forward to a vitamin-enriched, chromium-plated, starred-and-striped super-*Concorde*, which will carry twice as many people three times as fast on four times as many routes. Remember the *Comet*, which was *the* jet airliner until the *Boeing* came along? Fortunately it now appears that the *Concorde*, at least, is a dead duck; but not, it may be noted, on environmental grounds; purely on economic ones.

Why do we climb Mount Everest? Because it is there. Why do we send men to the moon? Because it, too, is there. The only difference is that the latter is a great deal more expensive; from the point of view of sheer futility it is hard to separate the two exercises. Suppose your house is falling down; the roof is leaking and the floorboards are rotten through. Is your response to this situation to mow the front lawn, or put a lick of paint on the window-sills, or prune the roses? I imagine not (unless, like me, you are too incompetent to fix the house yourself and too disorganized to get someone else to do it). But the space programme is strictly an exercise in rose-pruning while the house crashes to the ground. Again, all that can be said for it is that it shows what extraordinary progress we have made: we can spend billions of dollars sending three men to the moon in order to show how clever we are. By the same token, the fact that in the time it took the astronauts to fly to the moon and back, hundreds of thousands of people starved to death might be thought to reveal our inordinate stupidity. But going to the moon is progress; it's glamorous, prestigious, exciting; it's a splendid vision to spur us all on to greater things. Whether a few million more or less people starve is irrelevant to the operation. Of course it does not follow either that if the moonshots had never happened the money would have been spent on some more worthwhile project.

No one can deny that the space programme has had a lot of 'useful' results: telecommunications, weather forecasting, miniaturization. But they're all strictly rose-pruning. A well-fed, reasonably populated world could afford such rich men's follies; our present world cannot. But this, of course, is heresy; standing in the way of progress is just not playing the game. The need to strive onward, ever upward, is so deeply ingrained in us that, even if the rewards are now doubtful or non-existent, the urge is incapable of being switched off. So has it always been; so shall it continue. We shall lead the Tsembaga out of the error of his ways and bestow upon him all the benefits of a society which he has managed to escape up to now. Like Peter Matthiessen's Mart Quarrier[9] and Noël Coward's Uncle Harry, we shall 'lead the wretched heathen to the light'.[10] And, as Matthiessen also points out in his bewitching account of an anthropological expedition to study the Kurelu people of West Iran, 'the armed patrols and missionaries invaded their land on the heels of the expedition, and by the time this account of them is published, the proud and warlike Kurelu will be no more than another backward people, crouched in the long shadow of the white man.'[11]

This reminds us that not all of our glorious progress has been technological. Is it any coincidence that the religion of the supermen, the white technocrats, is Christianity? 'The victory of Christianity over paganism', writes Lynn White,[12] 'was the greatest psychic revolution in the history of our culture . . . Our daily habits of action . . . are dominated by an implicit faith in perpetual progress which was unknown to either Greco-Roman antiquity or to the Orient. It is rooted in, and is indefensible apart from, Judeo-Christian theology. The fact that Communists share it merely helps to show . . . that Marxism, like Islam, is a Judeo-Christian heresy'.

All this has some very significant consequences, as White goes on to point out. 'Like Aristotle, the intellectuals of the ancient West denied that the visible world had had a beginning. Indeed, the idea of a beginning was impossible in the framework of their cyclical notion of time. In sharp contrast, Christianity inherited from Judaism not only a concept of time as nonrepetitive and linear but also a striking story of creation.'

Hence one origin of the concept of perpetual progress. To quote from another respected source: 'the earth was without form, and void' and then God said 'Let there be light' and then 'Let the dry land appear' and let it 'bring forth grass . . . herb . . . and fruit tree' and 'the moving creature that hath life.'

Things were getting better all the time. But the final step in the creation story is one representing not only progress, but also domination: 'Let us make man in our own image . . . and let them have dominion over . . . all the earth, and every creeping thing that creepeth upon the earth . . . and God said unto them, Be fruitful, and multiply, and replenish the earth and subdue it: and have dominion over . . . every living thing that moveth upon the earth'.

Christianity is, then, 'the most anthropocentric religion the world has seen . . . Man shares, in great measure, God's transcendence of nature'. The earth was created entirely for the benefit of man, his plaything to do with as he wished. The philosophies which it replaced were, by contrast, usually forms of pagan animism in which 'every tree, every spring, every stream, every hill had its own . . . guardian spirit . . . Before one cut a tree, mined a mountain, or dammed a brook, it was important to placate the spirit in charge of that particular situation . . . By destroying pagan animism, Christianity made it possible to exploit nature in a mood of indifference' (White).

In similar vein, Masao Watanabe[13] has drawn attention to the contrast between Western and Eastern cultures which parallels the Christianity/pagan dichotomy. 'For the Japanese and for other Oriental peoples,' he notes, 'man was considered as a part of nature, and the art of living in harmony with nature was their wisdom of life.' On the Occidental idea of perpetual progress, he comments, 'In the Japanese view, there existed no . . . absolute "onceness" of time in the Western sense. Everything came and went in cycles.' But, he concludes, 'this kind of sentiment has been fading rapidly in Japan since the hasty introduction of modern science and technology . . . The Japanese people do not quite realize what is happening to nature and to themselves, and are thus . . . more helpless in the current environmental crisis.'

Of course it is not sheer luck that the most dominant and 'successful' societies are Christian. Christianity has triumphed because it happened at the right time to the right set of people; it encoded a system of values peculiarly apt for aggressive, expansionist groups. Robert Bigelow's[14] comments on the Old Testament account of the return to the promised land provide an illuminating parallel:

'Moses was well aware of the importance of discipline and co-operation within large armies . . . In the late second millenium BC . . . a multitude of Canaanites were bickering over good land in the Jordan valley, and a multitude of Israelites were bickering over poor land on the Sinai peninsula. The victors in the impending holocaust would be those who could most effectively suppress internal dissension within their own ranks. Moses proceeded to do this with great energy . . . . It was important to rally in large numbers under one god, since those who failed to do so were being slaughtered wholesale. In the nutcracker area between Egypt and Mesopotamia, warfare was a *religion*, in a very literal sense. The religion of Moses and Joshua was not an unusual one. The multitude of little gods differed mainly in the people they had chosen as their own. All of them were savage, all were parching with thirst for the blood of those who refused to worship them.'

And all that that goes to show is that we choose our religions to suit our purposes. There is a story, possibly apocryphal, of an Australian petrol company which one day analysed its petrol and found to its surprise that there was a large amount of a metallic element (let us call it octanium) in it. But they were nonplussed only momentarily; in no time at all they had started a new advertising campaign along the lines of: 'SUPER-GRADE SWINDLEJUICE: The Only Petrol with the Magic Additive OCTANIUM'. If you're stuck with it you may as well turn it to your advantage. If you want to encourage progress and domination you may as well adopt a religion which is based upon them.

Let's hear it for progress, then: technological progress is the magic additive which has made our lives easier and cured all our past ills; and technological progress is still the mass-appeal panacea of today. Hardy are the souls, such as Paul Ehrlich and John Holdren,[15] who say, 'In terms of the problem of feeding the world, for example, technological fixes suffer from limitations in scale, lead time, and cost . . . They are too little, too late, and too expensive . . . Even the most enlightened technology cannot relieve us of the necessity of grappling forthrightly and promptly with population growth.' Even braver the soul such as Garrett Hardin,[16] when he writes:

> 'It is fair to say that most people who anguish over the population problem are trying to find a way to avoid the evils of overpopulation without relinquishing any of the privileges they now enjoy. They think that farming the seas or developing new strains of wheat will solve the problem – technologically. I try to show here that the solution they seek cannot be found. *The population problem cannot be solved in a technical way*' [my italics].

(Hardin suggested in this paper that the solution lay in changes in human attitudes, i.e. in the political and moral spheres. A few issues of *Science* later there appeared a rejoinder[17] by a political scientist, hastily disclaiming that the social or political realms could offer any solutions, and passing the buck back to the natural scientists again.)

But the Ehrlichs and the Hardins are voices crying in the wilderness; we know perfectly well that there always have been, always will be, technological fixes. Anthony Storr[18] writes of aggression: there is 'the belief or hope that, if only society were better organized or children reared in ways which did not encourage them to be aggressive, men would live in peace with one another . . . It is . . . particularly characteristic of modern Americans to hold these opinions, since perennial optimism makes it hard for them to believe that there is anything unpleasant either in the physical world or in human nature which cannot be "fixed".'

Substitute *mankind* for *Americans*, and *impossible* for *hard*, and the nail has been hit on the head with deadly precision. And Arthur Koestler[19] provides us with the ultimate child-of-his-time solution to the whole ghastly mess: we shall simply take a pill. At the end of his long, thoughtful and mystical *The Ghost in the Machine*, he tells us that 'the most urgent task of biochemistry is the search for a remedy . . . a more sophisticated range of aids [i.e. drugs] to promote a co-ordinated, harmonious state of mind . . . a state of dynamic equilibrium in which thought and emotion are reunited . . .'

NOTES

1 RAPPAPORT, ROY. 'The Flow of Energy in an Agricultural Society', *Scientific American*, Vol. 224 (1971) 116-32
HANDLER, PHILIP (ed.). *Biology and the Future of Man* (Oxford University Press 1970)

2 WEBB, LEONARD. 'The Rape of the Forests', in: A. J. Marshall (ed.), *The Great Extermination* (London, Heinemann 1966)

3 ALEXANDER, R. D. 'The Search for an Evolutionary Philosophy of Man', *Proceedings of the Royal Society of Victoria*, Vol. 84 (1971) 99-120

4 'ROYAL COMMISSION OF INQUIRY INTO THE FAILURE OF THE WEST GATE BRIDGE.' Report (Government Printer, Melbourne 1971)

5 THOMAS, WILLIAM L. (ed.). *Man's Role in Changing the Face of the Earth* (University of Chicago Press 1956)

6 'SENATE SELECT COMMITTEE ON WATER POLLUTION.' *Water Pollution in Australia* (Commonwealth Government Printing Office, Canberra 1970)

7 WAGNER, RICHARD H. *Environment and Man* (New York, Norton and Company 1971)

8 BIERCE, AMBROSE. *The Devil's Dictionary* (Oxford, Dolphin Books 1911)

9 MATTHIESSEN, PETER. *At Play in the Fields of the Lord* (London, Heinemann 1965)

10 COWARD, NOEL. *The Lyrics of Noël Coward* (London, Heinemann 1965)

11 MATTHIESSEN, PETER. *Under The Mountain Wall* (London, Heinemann 1963)

12 WHITE, LYNN. 'The Historical Roots of Our Ecologic Crisis', *Science*, Vol. 155 (1967) 1203–7

13 WATANABE, MASAO. 'The Conception of Nature in Japanese Culture', *Science*, Vol. 183 (1974) 279-82

14 BIGELOW, ROBERT. *The Dawn Warriors* (London, Hutchinson 1969)

15 EHRLICH, PAUL R., and HOLDREN, JOHN. 'Impact of Population Growth', *Science*, Vol. 171 (1971) 1212-17

16 HARDIN, GARRETT. 'The Tragedy of the Commons', *Science*, Vol. 162 (1969) 1243-48

17 CROWE, BERYL L. 'The Tragedy of the Commons Revisited', *Science*, Vol. 166 (1969) 1103-7

18 STORR, ANTHONY. *Human Aggression* (London, Allen Lane: The Penguin Press 1968)

19 KOESTLER, ARTHUR. *The Ghost in the Machine* (London, Hutchinson 1967)

5 Down with Negative Feedback!

'These violent delights have violent ends.'
Shakespeare: *Romeo and Juliet*

Cybernetics is the science of communication and control within systems. One of the most important forms of control is feedback, where the product of some process influences (or 'feeds back to') the process itself. When you put your money in a savings bank it grows in quantity because of the operation of a positive feedback control. The process involved, of course, is the accumulation of interest on capital; and as interest is generated it becomes capital, which in turn generates interest which becomes capital, which in turn . . . All this means that your money grows at an increasing rate: the more of the product (interest) there is, the more the operation of the process (accumulation of interest on capital) is facilitated. Thus if you draw a graph of the amount of money in your account against time, you will find that not only does the curve slope upward, it slopes upward at an ever steeper angle.

If you put a yeast cell or a bacterium in a bottle of culture solution, and stand back to observe, you will see precisely the same feedback process operating (although of course it isn't nearly as interesting as watching your money grow). The one cell will become two, each of which will become two, each of which . . . and so on. The more products (cells) there are, the more the process (cell production by division) occurs. One, two, four, eight, sixteen, thirty-two, sixty-four . . . that is the arithmetic of positive feedback. It's a remarkably efficient growth process: a classic illustration is the old tale of the chap who did some potentate or other a favour, and was asked to name his reward. He modestly requested that he be given one grain of wheat for the first square of a chessboard, two for the second, four for the third, eight for the fourth, and so on up to the sixty-fourth . . . It turned out that what he was asking for ran into *millions of tons* of wheat. Apparently no one had told the potentate about The Power of Positive Feedback.

But positive feedback isn't the whole story of cybernetics. Perhaps you are one of the people who keeps a tropical aquarium: it provides us with an example of another kind of control process. You probably attempt to maintain the water in your aquarium at about 75°F (24°C): that is the 'desirable' temperature. What happens if there is a departure from this desirable level? – say the water gets cooler. What happens is that the lowered temperature causes a bimetallic strip in your aquarium thermostat to contract, thereby closing an electrical contact which turns the heater on. So the water heats up, but if it gets much above 75° the bimetallic strip expands, opens the contact, and turns off the heater. So the temperature drops again, until the thermostat . . . This is clearly a different kind of feedback operation. In this case, once there is a lot of the product (heat), the production process (generation of heat by the heater) is discouraged or stopped. But notice that it isn't stopped entirely; it is switched off only until the amount of product has dropped below the desirable level: and that starts the process up again. This is *negative* feedback: the amount of product regulates the rate of production, so that instead of an endless growth process we have an equilibrium resulting. (*Endless* growth is of course a rather loose phrase; in reality there can be no such thing.)

You are a walking maze of negative feedback loops. If you get too hot you sweat, which cools you; but if you get too cool you shiver, which warms you: your temperature keeps hovering around an equilibrium. If you have a lot of sugar in your blood the excess is converted into glycogen and stored in your liver (unless you are a diabetic). If your blood sugar level gets low, glycogen is reconverted into glucose: the 'set point' is restored. And so it goes on; it is all done so neatly that Walter Cannon entitled his book about such processes *The Wisdom of the Body*.

We may take as a general rule: where there is a biological process there will be feedback, and if we find any apparent exceptions we shall scrutinize them rather carefully. But we should first distinguish between two kinds of control system: *intrinsic* and *extrinsic* ones. Let's look at a child going along a street. If he is by himself his average speed is regulated intrinsically: if he goes too slowly he gets bored and speeds up; if he goes too fast he gets tired and slows down. The wisdom of his body is in command. But suppose he is walking with his mother. If he dawdles, she tells him to hurry up; if he dashes on ahead she calls on him to slow down and wait for her. Here his speed is being controlled extrinsically, by an agent outside himself.

This is quite an important distinction. What Wynne-Edwards was proposing (Chapter 3) amounted to an intrinsic mechanism of animal population control: a system operated by the population itself. We decided that this could not be so, because a population is no more than an arbitrary and incidental collection of individuals, and it cannot therefore have evolved functions of its own. This does not of course mean that negative feedback controls cannot operate on populations; only that if they do, they must be extrinsic ones.

Let's have another look at our yeast cell in a bottle; or rather 256, 512, 1,024, 2,048 or however many cells there are by this time. If we keep watching long enough we shall find that eventually the number stops growing. It may level off for a while, then it will start dropping, and, unless we intervene, it will plummet all the way back to zero. What has happened? Just this: the growing colony has run out of nutrients or space, or perhaps it's run into an accumulation of metabolic wastes. The intrinsic positive feedback loop has been suppressed by an extrinsic negative one. Cells began to reproduce less successfully or not at all; cells began to die and not be replaced. To the cells making up the population the sky is the limit, but the cells' environment imposes its own limit much earlier than that. Positive feedback is *always* supplanted by negative feedback sooner or later; it is part of the very nature of the finiteness of things. Thus no species can achieve an actual rate of increase anywhere near its potential rate; or, in financial terms again, no sum of money can be allowed to earn compound interest except for a very short time.[1]

We can translate the story of David Lack's robins into cybernetic language, too. The process in question is reproduction; and since each pair of robins lays ten eggs, we are dealing with positive feedback with a vengeance. If all eggs laid resulted in reproducing adults, the series would go 2, 10, 50, 250, 1,250, 6,250, 31,250 . . . On the other hand we know that in reality there is a population set point about which the number of robins fluctuates fairly narrowly. Lack[2] censused a population of robins at Dartington, South Devon, in April and December 1935, April and December 1936, April and December 1937, April 1938 and April 1945. The respective counts were 12, 11, 16, 17, 21, 15, 19, and 23. Over those ten years, then, the number nearly doubled. Yes, but think what it could have done, given the arithmetic sequence above. Clearly, in the final analysis, the rate of reproduction of robins is not controlled solely by positive feedback.

The fluctuations are, as Lack[3] points out, 'between limits that are extremely small when compared with what is theoretically possible'.

So negative feedback (extrinsic, by definition) must have a hand in the process; and we have in fact already looked at the nature of the negative feedback loop. Its component parts are inclement weather, predators, diseases and starvation. But note that not all of these are necessarily *absolute* controls: they do not invariably cull a given number of robins, year in and year out. Rather most of them are *density-dependent* controls: their effectiveness depends on how many robins there are. If there are a lot of robins around there is less food per robin, diseases spread faster, and predators may take a greater toll. Conversely, if there are few robins there is relatively more food, less likelihood of epidemic disease, and a lesser effect of predators. In the first case the number of robins will decrease; in the second it will increase. We may look upon the environment as having a 'carrying capacity' for robins, and it is this carrying capacity which fixes the level of the set point. It is negative feedback, in terms of survival or mortality, which keeps the population size fluctuating, within narrow limits, about the set point.

So there we are: we have looked at some of our Chapter 2 examples again in cybernetic terms, and we have come to precisely the same conclusions as we did before. And if we now apply our new terminology to the human situation, we shall again find the real difference between this population and those of other creatures. It is simply this: man's reproduction is, as we would expect, first and foremost under the control of an intrinsic positive feedback loop. Hence the birthday notices that one sometimes sees: Mr Methuselah Jones today celebrated his hundredth birthday. The birthday party was attended by ninety-two of his descendants, including seven children, eighteen grandchildren, fifty-five great-grandchildren and fourteen great-great-grandchildren. And this example also reveals what is different about man's system; he has removed the negative feedback control. He has prevented any set point from being established; the only point is a sliding one, and, so far, the only direction it has slid is upward. So we can identify another of the factors contributing to the self-destructive process. Man has adopted a no-negative-feedback, perpetual growth system as his philosophy of life, and he is the only element in the whole biosphere to have done so. His is a world in which negative feedback is anathema; 'Down with negative feedback!' is his rallying cry, and the insignia on his battle standard is an exponential curve rampant on a field of feedback loops, discarded.

Looked at in another way, man has succeeded in increasing the carrying capacity of the earth for men. He has removed most of the feedback controls such as predation and disease, and he has managed up to now to push the carrying capacity high enough to prevent starvation from exerting its negative control. Of course, achieving such a monumental and quite unprecedented boost in the earth's capacity has had some ghastly effects, and worse are yet to come. Nonetheless no one could argue that — if success is to be judged by the sheer weight of numbers — man has not been remarkably successful in his campaign of cybernetic defiance. Perpetual population growth has been an eminently satisfactory policy up to now; obviously there is reason enough to be sceptical about people who advocate population control. The fact that systems which are governed by positive feedback alone are destined to be short-lived is best either ignored, or firmly denounced as heresy.

There is also another factor operating here: man, like every other organism, has always behaved according to short-term goals and strategies. Basically his approach has been to do whatever is necessary to secure the good of himself and his children. It was never necessary to wonder whether this or that course would be more likely to achieve good for his grandchildren or great-grandchildren; largely because there was virtually nothing he could do which would influence his descendants directly. Life was a day-to-day, or at most a year-to-year, affair. Planning, yes; predictions based on probabilities, yes; but only in the short term. In general he had enough troubles keeping himself and his family intact without worrying about those who were to come later.

Now, of course, man finds himself in a position where what he does today is going to have enormous influence on future generations. The decision to drop atomic bombs on Hiroshima and Nagasaki left a legacy whose effects are still profound nearly thirty years later. The discovery of penicillin, of DDT, of the internal combustion engine, had effects which went far beyond the generation which discovered them. And the point is that most of these effects – and all the long-term ones – were entirely unpredicted. Jay Forrester[4] sums it up very well:

'Social systems usually exhibit fundamental conflict between the short-term and long-term consequences of a policy change. A policy which produces improvement in the short run is usually one which degrades the system in the long run . . . A series of actions all aimed at short-run improvement can eventually burden a system with long-run depressants so severe that even heroic short-run measures no longer suffice. Many of the problems which the world faces today are the eventual result of short-run measures taken over the last century.'

Man is simply not endowed with any capacity for long-term planning; he either refuses to do it or does it with hopeless inaccuracy. Recently there was a debate on Australian television between a proponent of Zero Population Growth and an opponent who believed that Australia should at least double its population as fast as possible. The gist of the opponent's argument was, 'If population growth continues at the present rate we shall still reach only *n* million by the end of the century; and of course it's ridiculous to try to plan further ahead than that.' One would have liked to point out (and even the ZPG man failed to) that if ZPG policies were instituted tomorrow the population would *still* be very close to *n* million by the year 2000; indeed, the whole argument is meaningless unless one bases it on the years *after* 2000. But that is too far away; there has never been any value in worrying about the future beyond tomorrow, or perhaps next year. When nearly one hundred British intellectuals were asked, between 1924 and 1932, to describe their vision of the future, none of them mentioned overpopulation, though the biologist J. B. S. Haldane was concerned about the dangers of underpopulation.[5] Aldous Huxley wrote in 1946 of his 1932 *Brave New World*[6], it 'is a book about the future and . . . a book about the future can interest us only if its prophecies look as though they might conceivably come true.' He goes on to apologize for not foreshadowing nuclear fission; one might now add that he did not foresee pollution, over-population, or mass starvation either. And Gordon Rattray Taylor, writing in 1968, is almost exclusively concerned in his *Biological Time Bomb*[7] with such trivia as organ transplantation, arrested death and the creation of life.

So: man judges the success or otherwise of his strategies entirely in terms of their short-term effects; he is not equipped to do it in any other way. He harpoons as many whales as he can this year, even though he knows full well that in the long term he is harpooning himself. That doesn't count: it's immediate results that matter. He sells as many of his stenching, fuming motor cars as he can today, although he knows that in the long term the more he sells the higher the pressures will mount to force him to make some other, and less disastrous, kind of car. And, in the even longer term, he also knows that each car built today is less iron ore remaining tomorrow, until one day there is none . . .

So is it too with the denial of negative feedback: the removal of feedback restraints from human population growth has been a spectacular, triumphant achievement in the short term. In the long term (if we may be allowed the luxury of a little heresy) the conquest of negative feedback is going to have some even more spectacular consequences. The result of declining child mortality today will be greatly increased child mortality tomorrow. The eradication of some kinds of disease today is the direct ancestor of other kinds of disease – kwashiorkor, beriberi, malnutrition – tomorrow. The freeway that carries us so fast and so comfortably today will be mourned tomorrow for what it really is: wilful destruction of arable land. And the luxury of being able to choose to have n children today will metamorphose into the horror of having $n+x$ grandchildren, or great-grandchildren, or whatever, die of starvation tomorrow.

But, it is instructive to note, so deeply ingrained is our determination to deny negative feedback its due that we have not been satisfied with perpetual growth of population alone. In many respects even that isn't fast enough for us. There are countless areas in our social and commercial systems where we have demanded an even faster growth rate than population expansion by itself can provide. After all, even if negative feedback isn't operating on the number of people, it does act in a half-baked sort of fashion on the quantities of resources those people require. There is a limit on resource consumption: the number of people that there are to do the consuming. Certainly it is true that this is an ever-growing number; but it's a growth rate of only about 0.5-4.0% per year (depending on where you live), which doesn't allow you to expand production and sales at anything like a satisfying rate. But of course there's an easy way around this annoying constraint, and we were quick to hit on it. If you can't have more people as fast as you want them, then you simply increase resource consumption per person; it's just as good a method for increasing growth rates. In other words, you remove the feedback loop from resource consumption by destroying the approximate parity between number of people and quantity of resources consumed. In some instances – food is an example – there is not a great deal you can do. You can increase only slightly the actual amount of food that people eat. But even in this case you can persuade them to eat less nutritious and more expensive foods which require more elaborate production and packaging; there's good profit in that. And for other commodities the limit is set only by your ingenuity. What you must do, if the market is showing signs of saturation with your product, is to alter or supplement or replace the product, so that you have created a new commodity which suddenly everybody needs all over again.

Laundry products are a shining example for all other manufacturers to follow. Time was when all you needed in your laundry was a packet of soap powder. Then suddenly you had to have detergents. They went through their own evolution in which bleaches, enzymes and other irrelevant additives came and went at breathtaking speeds, and everybody on the street had the whitest white. Or *thought* they had, until they discovered that they really needed a pre-wash soaker, too. A whole new market. And then they needed an after-wash rinse. And then different detergents for different fabrics. And then a cold-water detergent as well as a hot-water one. The growth rate was starting to look fairly respectable. And it's done with the simplest of techniques: all you have to do is to convince people (thoroughly well-off people) that they're not quite as well off as they might be, and they'll strive to raise their level of well-offness by buying any damnfool thing you can think of. As Dorothy L. Sayers[8] put it: 'Whatever you're doing, stop it and do something else! Whatever you're buying, pause and buy something different! Be hectored into health and prosperity. Never let up! Never go to sleep! Never be satisfied! If once you are satisfied, all our wheels will run down. Keep going – and if you can't, Try Nutrax for Nerves!'

Granted all this, it is nevertheless staggering just how easy it is to eliminate the nasty stagnation that is negative feedback. You can persuade healthy, well-fed people to buy millions of dollars' worth of totally useless vitamin supplements to cram into their healthy, well-fed children. You can sell people slimming pills with one hand and high-calorie foods with the other. You can gently hint that those who don't get enough exercise will die young, and they will promptly deduce that what they need to save them from their fate is a home gymnasium costing hundreds of dollars. And, in the unlikely event that they pay no heed and decide to die young regardless, you can always sell them a plot in a Garden of Remembrance.

But that's not the only approach. If you can't cajole them into buying something different they can often be talked into buying more of what they've already got, or exchanging what they have now for a new one (which is the same, only better). Vance Packard[9] notes many fine examples of this technique: wedding ring manufacturers doubled their sales simply by promoting the two-ring ceremony; eyeglass makers explained that eyeglasses, far from being mere aids to vision, were actually 'fashion accessories', so that you needed two or three or four pairs to match different outfits. In a few decades the desirable number of bathrooms per home has gone from o to 1 to 2 (and in Australia at present to 2½, the ½ being a W.C.). And so it goes on; we can run rings around negative feedback when we really try.

But we have already noted that control by positive feedback alone for more than a very short time is intolerable. Well, what happens to systems from which the negative feedback loops have deliberately been removed? Think of your aquarium. What happens if the thermostat packs up and the heater stays on? The water gets hotter and hotter; the fish begin to gasp at the surface; later they go into spasms of frantic activity; later still, they die. Of course in this case you can intervene and impose an extrinsic control by switching off the heater, if you realize in time what's happening.

What happens if we remove the negative feedback controls from a population? It explodes, as the rabbit did in Australia (in this case we removed the population from the controls). Once again we stepped in, as extrinsic cybernetic angels, and set about the rabbits with discases and poisons. But notice that the common denominator in these situations, aquaria and Australian rabbits, is violence, upheaval, revolution. If we fail to re-impose the lost feedback on the aquarium it is overtaken by chaos; it is converted from a life-supporting system into a saucepan. But we are doing equal violence by turning off the heater: we are confessing that our carefully devised system is a failure; we are abandoning one of our most sacred principles. And if we try to look at the rabbits from the rabbits' point of view we can appreciate the fix they were in: they were offered a choice of two paths, both culminating in wholesale death and destruction. Either somebody imposed a solution on them, such as myxomatosis, which would re-introduce feedback in the form of disease; or they would go on a little longer until another feedback control began to operate: starvation. Not a pleasant dilemma for a rabbit to be faced with; although of course they weren't in any position to make the choice for themselves.

We *are*. We face precisely this dilemma; or rather we refuse to face it; that doesn't mean it isn't there. We have locked ourselves into a system ruled by positive feedback control – of population, of resource use, of GNP, of everything. We, and we alone in the biotic world, have chosen growth in place of equilibrium as our mode of existence. Yet cybernetic principles insist that our way of doing things is, as a permanent fixture, *intolerable*: negative controls are going to have to re-appear. Perpetual growth has to be converted into perpetual equilibrium; this is not an ideal or policy – it is a bald, incontrovertible fact. Such a conversion has, for man, never been attempted; but we can deduce from our aquaria and our rabbits that it isn't going to be easy, or pleasant, or popular. Whichever way it comes about it is going to bring violence and upheaval such as the world has never seen.

Suppose, at the time we were learning to conquer epidemic disease, some far-seeing prophet had told us: 'Look – let me warn you of the consequences of what you are doing. Your eradication of disease now is going to cause untold misery and suffering among your descendants; and although you think you're decreasing the death rate you are actually *increasing* it.' Would we have believed him? Of course we wouldn't, but even if he had been able to convince us that he was right it would have made no difference to our behaviour. We would have earnestly explained to him that we had to do the best we could, on humanitarian grounds if no other; that we would look after today and trust that by tomorrow something would turn up to take care of any additional problems that happened along.

That this is true is amply demonstrated by our attitude today. I know of no case in which we have sacrificed an immediate benefit for the sake of a long-term one. On the

L.G.   D contrary, we strive endlessly to achieve more and more, greater and greater, short-term benefits even when it is abundantly clear that they will be long-term disasters. We are the rabbits to whom the question has been put: 'Myxomatosis now, or starvation later?', and with resounding unanimity we have chorused our reply: 'Starvation, every time!'. And for once we can be certain that we are going to get our wish.

Negative feedback has to be reinstated; growth has to be replaced by equilibrium; in Kenneth Boulding's[10] metaphor, a cowboy economy has to be replaced by a spaceman economy. I am not, as Boulding was, pleading with you to help bring the conversion about; I am simply telling you that it's going to happen, regardless of what you choose to think or do about it. Boulding was operating on the assumption that we can achieve equilibrium relatively painlessly, deliberately, of our own volition, by careful planning and revision of present policies. I grant that that is theoretically possible; on the other hand it is also theoretically possible that I could climb into the ring with Muhammad Ali and smash him into a pulp. If all we are interested in is theoretical possibilities then we can stop worrying; we can agree with the British physicist J. H. Fremlin[11] that in the year 2854 the earth could be supporting sixty thousand billion people. To this end the oceans would be roofed over, and the outer surface of the planet hermetically sealed and covered over continuously (land and sea alike) with a two thousand storey building. There would be eight tons of people per square metre of the earth's surface. Little exercise could be tolerated, but 'one could expect some ten million Shakespeares and rather more Beatles to be alive at any one time, so that a good range of television entertainment should be available' (Fremlin). It is sad to find that this tongue-in-cheek paradise, too, has death staring it in the face: it will be at the limit imposed by the earth's ability to dissipate heat. A few more people, and bang! (or whimper) there's an end to it.

Let's look for a moment at the theoretical possibility of a contrived and controlled achievement of an earthly equilibrium. What would be some of the things involved? Well, for a start: a fixed number of people; no increase allowed the world over: a global growth rate of nought per cent. That means setting a mean number of offspring per couple of a little over two. And everybody will agree: communists, nationalists, democracies, dictatorships, peasants, millionaires, Buddhists, Jehovah's Witnesses, Negroes, W.A.S.P.s, Arabs, Israelis, Idi Amin and Edward Kennedy. They'll also accept unanimously that both production and consumption are bad, evil, horrible; throughput of any kind is a no-no. Manufacturers will indulge in cut-throat competition to see who can sell the *least* of his product; governments will be bombarded with votes of no confidence unless they can honestly proclaim that they have achieved a *negative* growth rate. Builders will acknowledge that the only justifiable reason for building a new house is an old one falling down. Car makers will gracefully submit to a state of affairs in which they get to sell a new car only when an old one wraps itself around a lamp-post or crumbles into dust; and later to one in which the motor car is phased out as a significant part of our lives. And *we*, you and I, will gladly forgo our two bathrooms and our three TV sets, our motor mowers and our air conditioners, as well as most of what we like to call our 'inalienable rights'.*

These are the kinds of things which constitute the theoretical possibility of our reinstating negative feedback ourselves; of deliberately setting out to do it and seeing it through. The next step, obviously, is to list the characteristics

---

* For other ideas of what constitutes a recipe for survival see *How to be a Survivor* by Ehrlich and Harriman (Ballantine Books, 1971) and *A Blueprint for Survival* by the Editors of *The Ecologist* (Penguin Books, 1972).

of our behaviour in the past which suggest that we have the capacity to turn the theory into reality. Let's list the countries which have launched successful birth control programmes and stuck to them for ever after. Let's list the nations which have announced that they've stopped trying to increase their GNP. Let's list the governments which in a single term of office have enacted *hundreds* of electorally unpopular acts and survived. Let's list the companies which are ready, willing and able to switch over to new production schedules which cater for a stable market. And the racial groups who get along together in perfect peace and harmony, sharing the same ideals, values and privileges.

Or perhaps we don't need to make lists. Let's just look instead at the United Nations Conference on the Human Environment held in Stockholm recently. Here at last was a chance for the world to show its unanimity; to reveal its overpowering passion to bring back feedback, to usher in equilibrium. Of course most of the Eastern Bloc didn't show up because East Germany wasn't invited to attend; and that is a far more serious disaster than the fact that the earth on which both Eastern and Western Blocs live is in an advanced state of decay. And many of the people who did attend pointed out that the conference had its priorities all wrong: the most significant of man's present problems is undoubtedly the *Concorde.* Or the structure of the European Economic Community. Or the Vietnam War. Or You Name It, We'll Demonstrate About It. The Australian delegate to the conference, on the other hand, showed that he really meant business: he got to Stockholm by car, aeroplane and taxi; but once he was there he rode around on a bicycle to do his bit for saving the environment. An action worthy of his portfolio; he was, would you believe, the Federal Minister for the Environment, Aborigines and the Arts; which I have also heard called the Ministry for Dealing with Things that

Ought to be Killed.

Jam today or jam tomorrow? – what has our traditional answer been? But that isn't even the question any more: those are two alternatives which we aren't offered. *No* jam tomorrow or *no* jam next week? – that is the question; and of course we have selected the only wise and sensible answer to it. As masters of the earth the choice was ours to make, and we made it honestly, forthrightly, unhesitatingly. All that happened is that the circumstances surrounding the choice have changed. If you live on a small island and keep goats how should you make your decision about the number of goats to keep? If goats die only of old age or when you slaughter one to eat you'll need to be pretty careful, or you'll end up with a plague of goats which will strip the island bare. So don't let the goats breed too freely. But what if the island is also inhabited by a pack of wolves which eat goats as fast as you can breed them? In this case you must obviously do your damnedest to produce as many goats as you possibly can, just to be sure of having one or two for yourself.

We live on an island, Earth, that once was full of wolves. But we have shot nearly all the wolves now, and nobody has explained to us that their name was Negative Feedback, and their consequence, Stability.

NOTES

1 HARDIN, GARRETT. 'The Cybernetics of Competition: A Biologist's View of Society', *Perspectives in Biology and Medicine*, Vol. 7 (1968) 58-84
2 LACK, DAVID. *The Life of the Robin* (London, Collins 1965)
3 LACK, DAVID. *Population Studies of Birds* (Oxford University Press 1966)

4 FORRESTER, JAY W. *World Dynamics* (Chichester, Wright-Allen Press 1971)

5 HARDIN, GARRETT. '1960: Cassandra Gets a Hearing', in: Garrett Hardin (ed.), *Population, Evolution and Birth Control* (Reading, W. H. Freeman 1969)

6 HUXLEY, ALDOUS. 1932. *Brave New World* (London, Penguin Books, 1955)

7 TAYLOR, GORDON RATTRAY. *The Biological Time Bomb* (London, Thames & Hudson 1968)

8 SAYERS, DOROTHY L. *Murder Must Advertise* (London, Gollancz 1933)

9 PACKARD, VANCE. *The Waste Makers* (London, Longmans, Green 1961)

10 BOULDING, KENNETH. 1966. 'The Economics of the Coming Spaceship Earth', in: Garrett Hardin (ed.), *Population, Evolution and Birth Control* (Reading, W. H. Freeman 1969)

11 FREMLIN, J. H. 'How Many People Can the World Support?', *New Scientist*, Vol. 24 (1964) 285–87

6 The Art of Delusion

'Human kind cannot bear very much reality.'
> T. S. Eliot: *Burnt Norton*

Hallowe'en Night 1938 was a memorable one in the USA.[1] On that night Orson Welles and his Mercury Theatre of the Air on the Columbia Broadcasting System presented an adaptation of a novel by his phonetic namesake, H. G. Wells. The novel was *War of the Worlds*, and so vivid was the dramatization that about seventeen per cent of the people who heard it took it seriously. At least a million people were convinced that Martian war machines had landed in New Jersey and were storming across the country, destroying everything in their path with their death rays and poison gas. People wept, or prayed, or bundled up their sleeping children and loaded them into their cars for a fast getaway. Telephone exchanges ran hot with farewell calls to relatives, and requests for information from radio stations, newspapers and police. One man used the money he had been saving for a new pair of shoes to buy a long-distance bus ticket; later he wrote a rather testy letter to a team of psychologists inquiring into the fracas, asking them to 'please have someone send me a pair of black shoes, size 9-B'.

The revealing thing is that, of the people who believed the play to be a genuine news broadcast, between a third and a half made no attempt whatever to verify their belief. They didn't tune to another radio station, or check with a neighbour, or phone the police. This is as much a tribute to man's prodigious gullibility as it is to Welles' dramatic brilliance. And in this lies the real moral of the story: what men believe is not a simple matter of black or white, fact or fiction, truth- or falsehood. The relationship between reality and human belief must be one of the least direct ones on record. It is easy *now* to look back at the Wells/Welles brainchild of 1938 and laugh at the simpletons who swallowed it so readily. It is much harder – it is close to impossible – to acknowledge that we now accept far more preposterous concoctions than this every day. We have woven for ourselves an inordinately complicated web in which reality is not merely obscured; it is forcibly prevented from rearing its head. It is a truism that people will believe just about anything you tell them; a truism which vast numbers of men have been quick to exploit in their dealings with other groups of men. This insatiable capacity to be deluded has vast and varied consequences, and not least among them is the almost complete lack of action on the problems that Commoner, Ehrlich, Hardin and all the others keep telling us about.

There are two main ways in which the system works, and both of them are well exemplified by the art of advertising. Suppose you come up with some new product which you really, seriously, believe does a certain job better than any of its competitors. It so happens that you are quite wrong, but you don't know that. To sell the thing you will advertise it as the best possible product, and myriads of people will buy it. Of course both you and they are suffering from a delusion, but that hardly matters. Your faith in your product is so overwhelming that you can easily rationalize the occasional doubts and odd disconcerting results; the consumer, likewise, is readily convinced by the tenacity with which you insist upon your delusion. So: the delusions of one man become the delusions of many.

On the other hand you may, before you reach the marketing stage, realize that your super-product is, after all, a flop. Your skills and special knowledge enabled you to carry out a series of performance tests, and they showed that your product was no better – perhaps it was somewhat worse – than its competitors. But need that make any difference? Of course not. The consumer lacks background knowledge, lacks expertise, and the chances are excellent that if you tell him the thing is the best, he'll happily believe you. He cannot be expected to know any better. So in this case a delusion is being fostered and spread by someone who is himself immune to it.

It makes no difference; the point is that however they get started, delusions travel like wildfire. We have already noted that man's talent for deluding himself is of considerable advantage to him; as Hardin[2] says: 'The emerging history of population is a story of disaster and denial – disaster foreseen, but disaster psychologically denied in our innermost being.' Our innermost being has had a long evolutionary history, a history in which it has very rarely been advantageous to heed the prophets of doom. Of course Noah's achievement constitutes a significant exception; but for a glance at the other side of the coin take Mhlakaza and his niece, Nongquause. She was a South African Xhosa girl who, in 1856, saw visions indicating that the destiny of the Xhosa people was to rise up and drive the white man out of the country. To this end the Xhosa would first have to slaughter all their own cattle and destroy all their own grain; once this was done the sun would turn blood-red and a great wind would spring up and sweep the white men away. Then the ghosts of dead warriors would arise and bring fat cattle, and the Xhosa would feast and rejoice . . .

The Xhosa were disheartened, already beaten in battle, dispossessed of their land, bitter, frustrated; perhaps that is why they heeded Nongquause's instructions. And by the time the great day came, in February 1857, 25,000 of them had starved to death; thousands more poured into the white man's Cape Colony, seeking not war but food . . . the population of British Kaffraria plummeted from over 100,000 to 37,000.[3]

Selection works powerfully against those who heed the Nongquauses of their time. 'It can't happen here' and 'I'm all right, Jack' are not merely amusing illustrations of human cussedness; first and foremost they express man's overwhelming desire to be given a delusion to believe in. All we ask is an unsinkable *Titanic* to pin our faith on, and when it sinks nothing will satisfy us but that another one be provided. Consider the Aberfan disaster in Wales in October 1966; more than a hundred children buried beneath the waste material from a coal mine; the slag heap suddenly, without warning, pouring down upon Pantglas Junior School.[4] Without warning? . . . Slag heaps had been sliding into Welsh valleys for years. It was widely known that provision had to be made for drainage of such heaps . . . the Aberfan one was undrained. It was strictly recommended that slag heaps should not exceed 20 feet in height . . . the one at Aberfan towered more than 100 feet before its collapse. But . . . 'it can't happen here'.

Man is an incurable optimist; it is relatively easy to make him believe things that he likes believing; as Francis Bacon put it, 'What a man had rather were true he more readily believes'. From this fact stems the whole glorious, tangled, Gordian system of communications that we now find ourselves saddled with. Virtually all the information input that we receive is filtered, diluted, supplemented or slanted; we are allowed to know only what others want us to know; to believe what others want us to believe. Our channels have become fuzzed up; the golden rule of our system is: transmit anything you like, as long as it's not reality. We simply do

not possess the means of rational, unbiased information trans-
fer. Very little of what you read or hear bears anything
more than a passing resemblance to the truth. There are
areas, of course, in which this fact is widely recognized: war
reporting is an example. Everyone tacitly accepts that 'South
Vietnamese Troops Capture 27 Red Tanks' probably means
in reality that a South Vietnamese soldier commandeered a
bicycle suspected to have once belonged to a Viet Cong sym-
pathizer's mother-in-law. Have you ever had the experience
of skipping through an encyclopaedia or some such, and
thinking, 'This is rather good', until you get to a section
dealing with a subject that you know a bit about? And you
find that that section is a load of codswallop. And has it then
struck you that by the same token the whole thing is probably
codswallop? The point is that the encyclopaedia does not
need to be accurate; that is not one of its functions. And
how many times have you heard an interview with a politician
that goes something like this? –

Interviewer: And are you therefore advocating withdrawal
   of the subsidy?

Minister: It's not a question of what we are advocating. My
   government has a policy, and, I might add, has had for
   some time, a policy, or policies, under which, when there
   is a question of a subsidy, as in this case, our policy is to
   examine the question in the light of our current thinking
   on subsidy policies . . .

I: Yes, but excuse me . . . are you going to withdraw it?

M: I beg your pardon . . . withdraw what?

I: The subsidy.

M: Now . . . wait a moment . . . I don't like that word
   withdraw in this context My own personal view, speaking
   for myself, of course – but let me hasten to add that my
   government's view is quite unanimous on this point – is
   that, in the current climate of thinking at this time – and

we have stated this quite explicitly both within and outside the House – we must maintain a flexible response capability in regard both to questions of policy, such as the one you raise, and questions . . .

I: So you are going to withdraw it?

M: Now there you go again – putting words into my mouth. As I was about to say, in questions of policy my government's policy is, and I think I may say always has been, that insofar as it is possible, given current considerations, our policy should be – and subsidies are only one example of this, and by no means the most important example – that whenever it is feasible, we should always strive to decide the question . . .

I: I'm afraid we're out of time, Mr Minister. Thank you very much.

Same thing again: there are no rewards for saying anything which might remotely be construed as useful or informative; *ergo*, it doesn't happen.

Let me quote another example, from an advertisement in a morning newspaper. It concerned electric clothes dryers, and it assured me that, among other things, there was a model of clothes dryer which was 'just right for my laundry'. Now (*a*) how the hell do they know I've got a laundry? and (*b*) allowing that I have, how come they can tell me so confidently what is going to fit into it? Do they know it better than I do? If I go and tell them that no clothes dryer with dimensions other than $1\frac{1}{2}$ inches x $1\frac{1}{2}$ inches x 17 feet will fit into it, will they smile charmingly and produce a model with exactly those dimensions? Later in the advertisement they informed me that the great thing about clothes dryers is that you can dry your clothes indoors, 'away from all the smoke and dust and pollution'. Are they seriously trying to tell me they're unaware that a goodly proportion of the dust, smoke and what-have-you is caused by the generation of electricity to power their fool clothes dryers? And another advertisement in the same paper trumpeted that driving such-and-such a car was 'A Great Way to Move'. Are they worried that if they didn't inform me of this I might rush out and invest in a car which represented a great way to stand still? No matter: the point of the examples is merely to show that we live in a world in which this sort of glorified twaddle is the norm; it is so thoroughly accepted that it goes without comment.

The crux of the matter is this: there is very rarely any pay-off to be had for either facing or propounding reality; there are, on the other hand, generous rewards for deluding yourself and others. This is not surprising, or horrifying, or despicable; it is simply inevitable. There is no point in crusading about it: you might just as well go on a crusade to abolish speech altogether. It is an integral part of our unique system of learned, symbolic language; you can't have the one without the other. If, way back there in the early pages of *African Genesis*, there had been two sorts of australopithecines: those who learned to delude themselves and their fellows, and those who didn't, you have only to ask: which group would have been more successful? G. L. Stebbins[5] has a relevant comment:

'Judging from the folkways and customs of "primitive" people, self-deception about the causes of natural phenomena was an accepted way of life over tens of thousands of years . . . If phenomena like the phases of the moon, the passage of the seasons, and the basis of thunder and lightning could not be explained, the invention of a god who was responsible for each phenomenon was an easy and acceptable deception that could replace the impossible solution.'

Which just goes to show that nothing has changed all that much.

'The notable thing about *human* behaviour is that it is learned. Everything a human being does as such he has had to learn from other human beings.'

'It is highly improbable that any form of man was ever characterized by [an inborn territorial] drive. Arguments based on fish, birds and other animals are strictly for them. They have no relevance for man.'

'Man is man because he has no instincts, because everything he is and has become he has learned, acquired, from his culture . . .'

'The fact is, that with the exception of the instinctoid reactions in infants to sudden withdrawals of support and to sudden loud noises, the human being is entirely instinctless.'

See what I mean? As nice a little bundle of delusions as ever you could hope to find. And those words were written, in case you are wondering, not in 1948 but in 1968, by M. F. Ashley Montagu[6] of Columbia University. If you believe that man lacks any innate tendencies to behave in certain ways then you're in a very comfortable position: everything can be 'fixed'. We admit that there are wars, yes; and there are ghettoes and racism, certainly; and pollution and starvation; no one could deny it. But they're all products of our culture, you see; and all we've got to do is to fix up our culture a bit here and there and bingo! – it'll be roses, roses all the way. For some reason or other what we've done is this: we've picked a culture that doesn't seem to suit us very well. It makes us do all sorts of nasty things like killing each other and exploiting each other and kicking each other about. But it's all *cultural*, you see, and cultural problems obviously have cultural solutions. It's simply a question of more education, better social services, a television set in every home . . . Give us more money, give us better research facilities, and we shall straighten out the world.

Montagu is worried by Ardrey's[7] and Lorenz's[8] ideas about man having innate aggressive propensities; he doesn't like to contemplate himself in those terms. The depth of his feeling is well shown by this sentence: 'As the reader will be able to judge for himself, the experts have found the theories of Ardrey and Lorenz unsound'. In other words: judge the issue for yourself, but just in case you're in any doubt, Lorenz and Ardrey are *wrong*. Note also the comforting reference to *the experts*: rest assured that us scientific whizzes have the matter well in hand; there's no need for you to worry about it. Perhaps Montagu's wrestlings with the problem of instinct need not concern us here, but they are representative of one of our Grand Delusions: the cultural (or technological) panacea. Here's another nice example (written, admittedly, in 1958, but none of Colin Clark's later writings suggest that he has altered his opinions):

> 'Countries the population of which has outrun their agricultural resources can industrialize, and exchange manufactures for imported food, as did Britain and Japan, and as India can – if they have a large population and a good transport system . . . This solution, however, is not open to the smaller and more isolated islands, away from the main channels of world trade. If they become crowded they must seek relief in emigration . . .'[9]

See how easy it is? Britain industrialized, so the world can. End of starvation. When countries get crowded they can export surplus people. End of overpopulation. And notice how blandly it ignores the whole problem: what of a world where there *is* no food to be imported in exchange for manufactures? And a world where nobody will accept other countries' emigrants because they have too many people of their own already?

Clark continues:

'We may take as our standard that of the most productive farmers in Europe, the Dutch, who feed 385 people per sq. km. of farm land, or 365 if we allow for the land required to produce their timber. Applying these standards throughout the world, as they could be with adequate skill and use of fertilizers, we find the world capable of supportinb 38 billion* people . . .'

Paul Ehrlich[10] has called this 'the Netherlands fallacy'. As he points out:

'The Netherlands actually requires large chunks of the earth's resources and vast areas of land not within its borders to maintain itself. For example, it is the second largest . . . importer of protein [per head of population] in the world, and it imports 63 per cent of its cereals, including 100 per cent of its corn and rice. It also imports all of its cotton, 77 per cent of its wool, and all of its iron ore, antimony, bauxite, chromium, copper, gold, lead, magnesite, manganese, mercury, molybdenum, nickel, silver, tin, tungsten, vanadium, zinc, phosphate rock (fertilizer), potash (fertilizer), asbestos and diamonds. It produces energy equivalent to some 20 million metric tons of coal and consumes the equivalent of over 47 million metric tons.'

* The word is used here in the American sense, i.e. a thousand million.

So there's another delusion gone, and what's the logical response to that? Find 'yet another, of course: 'In the very distant future, if our descendants outrun the food-producing capacity of the Earth, and of the sea, they will by that time be sufficiently skilled and wealthy to build themselves artificial satellites to live on' (Clark).

This is getting into the realms of the grandest of grand delusions. Even such an avowed denier of reality as Clark must, in the end, acknowledge that the world he is dealing with is a finite one; in other words, that somewhere, eventually, there *is* a limit to the number of people it can support. But to that little dilemma, too, he has a scientific solution: we'll simply increase the effective size of the earth.

It has been remarked that one of the few tangible benefits of the space programme has been that it has shown us our world for what it really is: a rather small, thoroughly finite ball of rock floating along in a vast, inhospitable, lifeless void. Maybe so, but that benefit is outweighed, I think, by a simultaneous disadvantage: man's 'conquest' of the moon has further bolstered our blind faith in the wizardry of Science. Anybody you care to ask will tell you that, Yes, man has now lived on the moon. We didn't need to build nearby, small, artificial satellites to live on; we just got right up and flew to that bigger, more distant, natural one. Today the moon; tomorrow . . . Who knows? 'Our children's children,' writes Erich von Däniken[11] in his ponderous science-fiction comedy *Chariots of the Gods?*, 'will go on interstellar journeys . . .' 'The moon,' says my encyclopaedia, 'has negligible atmosphere . . . its temperatures vary greatly . . . it is a dead world without water.' And despite all that, we have now lived there.

We have not, of course, lived on the moon in any sense of the word *live* as it applies on earth. What the astronauts (another nice delusion: they never have, and never will, 'sail to a star') really did was to take a piece of earth environment with them to the moon, and they were damned careful never to step outside it. If that is living on the moon, well, OK, we can stop worrying. In those terms we can also 'live' at the bottom of the oceans, the top of Mount Everest, the middle of the Sahara Desert, and pretty well anywhere else you care to name.

Garrett Hardin[12] has crisply disposed of the possibility that we can ever expect to live anywhere in the universe apart from this one little planet that we now inhabit. The other planets in our solar system can be dismissed out of hand as potential homes for mankind; each of them lacks two or more of the minimum requirements for human sustenance: a breathable atmosphere, a moderate temperature, a reasonable amount of water, and a bearable gravity. So we must look beyond the solar system to the stars to house our teeming millions. The nearest star, as any SF fan knows, is Alpha Centauri, and using one of our present moon-rockets it would take a mere 129,000 years to get there . . . But Alpha Centauri lacks planets, and we must therefore look further, to Barnard's Star, which is forty per cent further away again . . .

The real triumph (apart, of course, from the political and military propaganda angles) of the moonshots was the construction of a container which could carry a life-support system for three men so far, through such hostile conditions, and bring them safely home again. That's all it is: an academic, ivory-tower triumph. It has precisely nothing to do with the problem of finding homes for people to live in.

Of course we don't need any good-of-mankind rationale for messing about in spaceships; we can pursue the stars unhampered by any thoughts of reality. There is a whole science of *exobiology*: that is to say, the study of life outside the earth; indeed, we are already hard at work on the problem of communicating with this life. The two closest stars to us with a reasonable chance of having life-bearing planets are Epsilon Eridani and Epsilon Indi, respectively 10.8 and 11.3 light years away[13] (of course we don't *know* that they have planets at all, but it's a fair bet). Reluctantly we must allow that the probability of our visiting the neighbourhood of either of these stars is close enough to zero to make no difference. The physicist Edward Purcell[14] has dryly devised the best possible way of trying: a rocket powered by matter-antimatter. We could do the round trip, Epsilon Indi and back, in twenty-seven years in such a rocket. Of course, to carry a ten-ton payload the rocket would have to weigh 400,000 tons to start with (half matter and half antimatter). And to achieve enough acceleration our craft would have to radiate about 10^{18} watts near the beginning of its journey; an amount which turns out to be only a little more than the total power the earth receives from the sun. The radiation would consist of gamma rays, and it would kill not only everyone in the rocket, but everyone left on earth as well.

But don't give up hope: we can still try to communicate by signals. We could send a ten-word telegram a distance of twelve light years for a mere dollar's worth of electricity. Which *still* leaves one problem unsolved: what the hell are we going to say? Don't worry, we're working on it. There are also those who argue that since we're not too sure about what to transmit, the best thing is just to listen to the stars. We've got that well in hand, too; unfortunately up to now nobody out there has thought it worthwhile to say anything to us. (I confidently expected a message which ran, 'Hello Earth! Hello Earth! Epsilon Eridani Alpha calling! Look, we're crowded as hell and starving to death up here – you got room for a few more chaps?')

In our consideration of feedback processes we concluded that we can anticipate the forcible re-imposition of negative feed-back controls on our growth-happy world; a process whereby growth will be converted into equilibrium. Now one of the forces militating against the deliberate achievement of equilibrium is advertising. Advertising is a buy-more, consume-more, pollute-more philosophy; we should be busting our guts to buy, consume, pollute, less and less. The only sort of advertising which strikes me as being very reasonable from this point of view is that for tobacco and alcohol and other drugs. These are substances which tend to decrease your libido, lower your fertility, shorten your life-span, and generally reduce the magnitude of the disaster which you, as a human being on earth in the 1970s, represent: they're the answer to the earth-crusader's prayer. Needless to say, advertising for these products is just about the only kind that we are discouraging or banning.

It all comes back again to the question of motives, of pay-offs. The function of advertising is to make money for somebody or other; its motive is therefore clearly not to inform us of the truth. Likewise, all too often, the newspaper reporter: his motive is to stay in his job, and to achieve this he must write 'good' (i.e. sensational, controversial, newsworthy) stories. They need only enough of a ring of truth about them to relate them to real times and places; the rest is do-what-you-will. 'More than a hundred people' is *a hundred and one people* (or, more often, seven or twelve or twenty-three people); 'unofficial reports' is *my guess*; 'heavy casualties' is *somebody stubbed his toe*. Scientific literature is perhaps freer of these subterfuges, but it is by no means immune. Every budding scientist learns his correct publication jargon: 'It is generally accepted' means *I think*; 'Typical results are shown' means *the best results are shown*; 'accidentally strained during mounting' means *dropped on the floor*; 'handled with extreme care throughout the experiment' means *not dropped on the floor*; and so on.

So we have identified another of the peculiar features of man's biological nature: the necessity for him to be dosed daily with a generous spoonful of deception. We have seen how the consequences of this fact extend into every aspect of his life and social institutions. We have noted that motives for deluding oneself and others are legion; we have searched almost in vain for instances where there is a pay-off to be had for facing reality. We have looked at a variety of examples, but through them all runs a thread, and the thread is this: people prefer to believe things that give them a feeling of comfort and security. They will not accept things which make them feel unhappy, or guilty, or helpless. So the golden rule is: if the facts are disturbing, translate them into another form which is less disturbing. We might call this the art of the psychological euphemism, and it is one of the many extraordinary arts we have perfected. It is, I presume, the major reason for the success of Alvin Toffler's *Future Shock*.[15] If you, like I, took the *Future* to be an adjective, you probably thought when you picked up the book that it would be a nice, juicy catalogue of the ingredients of doomsday. But no: *Future* is a noun, and the book is simply about technical and social changes and the effects they have on us. The crises that face us are, in the main, fun things like over-choice, the rise of ad-hocracy, the trials of being a jet-setter, and so on. Not that Toffler does not have some important things to say: his discussion of our technocratic myopia, for instance, is superb. But his major canvases of the future are painted in hues of comparative triviality. They are exciting, entertaining, often amusing; but they are rarely horrifying, heart-breaking, soul-shattering. And that is why we went out in our millions and purchased *Future Shock*.

(One may question, incidentally, whether even Toffler's mini-crises rest upon very firm foundations. His concept of overchoice, for example, describes the kind of situation where the purchaser of a car must decide between umpteen dozen 'different' models because of the availability of 'options'. But it is naïve to identify this as real or substantial diversity and to base a psychological crisis of 'overchoice' upon it. The real trend, of course, is towards uniformity; but manufacturers, because of the sales advantage it gives them, have been quick to cover this all-embracing monotony with a paper-thin veneer of variety. There is far less *real* choice now about your mode of transport than there was in the days when the four-in-hand and the horseless carriage were fighting it out.)

Here's a more mundane example: there exists a series of incredibly deadly poisons which no right-thinking person would allow within a mile of him if he knew what they really were. Their names are DDT, endrin, dieldrin, aldrin, telodrin, chlordane, endosulphan, methoxychlor, heptachlor, diazinon, parathion, dichlorvos . . . Now we are all aware that these chemicals are an ecological nasty; the point of the example resides in the name we have chosen to bestow on them: *pesticides*, things that kill pests. If we had even a half-baked streak of realism in us we would call them *biocides*, destroyers of life. We would fairly describe them (many of them, at any rate) as substances which are lethal to all living organisms, including man; and which may in sublethal doses have long-term chronic effects on humans and other animals. But of course if you put all that on the label everyone would feel so uncomfortable that they wouldn't buy the things, and then where would you be? So, *pesticides* it is. (By the same token you could sell high-powered rifles as *birdkillers* – or you'd be more likely to say *avicides* – and on those grounds encourage everyone to use one in his own back yard. Of course, you'd say, they *can* kill people, but that's not the purpose they're marketed for.)

John Maddox[16] makes extensive use of the technique of calling nasty things by nice names; and, once you realize this, he becomes one of the most frightening of all the prophets of doom. He raises the same bogeys as everyone else but then dismisses them with irrelevant comments, leaving the spectres dangling there, unallayed, before your eyes. Thus, in commenting on the growth of Europe's population from 300 million in 1950 to 455 million in 1968, he writes: 'In other words, more than 70 million people have failed to die in childhood or early adulthood, but instead have survived to contribute to the economy of Europe. Does such an increase, for such a benign reason, justify the name population explosion?' (What name should we give it? How about Escalation, Numbers-Wise, of Hominid Organismal Units? Will that lessen the impact?)

Or again: 'It is salutary to remember that the great whales of the South Atlantic have been killed off by over-fishing, not by pollution.' Apparently that somehow makes them less dead.

On a variation of the same theme, if you are confronted with a problem that you are powerless to solve, transmute it into one that you *can* handle, or at least not feel guilty about; you will then be able to sit back and relax again. Garrett Hardin[17] has brought this one home to us with his usual clarity, in a *Science* editorial in February 1971:

'I was in Calcutta when the cyclone struck East Bengal in November 1970. Early dispatches spoke of 15,000 dead, but the estimates rapidly escalated to 2,000,000 and then dropped back to 500,000. A nice round number: it will do as well as any, for we will never know. The nameless ones who died . . . left no trace of their existence. Pakistani parents repaired the population loss in just 40 days, and the world turned its attention to other matters.

What killed those unfortunate people? The cyclone, newspapers said. But one can just as logically say that overpopulation killed them. The Gangetic delta is barely above sea level. Every year several thousand people are killed in quite ordinary storms. If Pakistan were not over-crowded, no sane man would bring his family to such a place. Ecologically speaking, a delta belongs to the river and the sea; man obtrudes there at his peril . . .

Were we to identify overpopulation as the cause of a half-million deaths, we would threaten ourselves with a question to which we do not know the answer: *How can we control population without recourse to repugnant measures?* Fearfully we close our minds to an inventory of possibilities. Instead we say that a cyclone caused the deaths, thus relieving ourselves of responsibility for this and future catastrophes. "Fate" is *so* comforting . . .

No one ever dies of overpopulation. It is unthinkable.'

NOTES

1 CANTRILL, HADLEY. *The Invasion from Mars* (Princeton University Press 1940)

2 HARDIN, GARRETT. 'Introduction', in: Garrett Hardin (ed.), *Population, Evolution and Birth Control* (Reading, W. H. Freeman 1969)

3 MARQUARD, LEO. *The Story of South Africa* (London, Faber & Faber 1955)

4 TIDMARSH, SHEILA. *Disaster* (London, Penguin Education 1969)

5 STEBBINS, G. L. 'The Natural History and Evolutionary Future of Mankind', *The American Naturalist*, Vol. 104 (1970) 111-126

6 MONTAGU, M. F. ASHLEY. *Man and Aggression* (Oxford University Press 1968)

7 ARDREY, ROBERT. *The Territorial Imperative* (London, Collins 1966)

8 LORENZ, KONRAD. *On Aggression* (London, Methuen 1966)
9 CLARK, COLIN. 'World Population', in: Garrett Hardin (ed.), *Population, Evolution and Birth Control* (Reading, W. H. Freeman 1969)
10 EHRLICH, PAUL R., and HOLDREN, JOHN. 'Impact of Population Growth', *Science*, Vol. 171 (1971) 1212-17
11 VON DANIKEN, ERICH. *Chariots of the Gods?* (London, Souvenir Press 1969)
12 HARDIN, GARRETT. 'Interstellar Migration and the Population Problem', *Journal of Heredity*, Vol. 50 (1959) 68-70
HARDIN, GARRETT. *Biology: Its Principles and Implications* (Reading, W. H. Freeman 1966)
13 SNEATH, P. H. A. *Planets and Life* (London, Thames & Hudson 1970)
14 PURCELL, EDWARD. Quoted by NEWMAN, JAMES R., 'Communicating with Intelligent Life Elsewhere in the Universe', in: Garrett Hardin (ed.), *Science, Conflict and Society* (Reading, W. H. Freeman 1969)
15 TOFFLER, ALVIN. *Future Shock* (London, The Bodley Head 1970)
16 MADDOX, JOHN. *The Doomsday Syndrome* (London, Macmillan 1972)
17 HARDIN, GARRETT. 'Nobody Ever Dies of Overpopulation', *Science*, Vol. 171 (1971) Editorial

7 More Lights that Failed

'For a bright manhood, there is no such word as *fail*.'
Edward Bulwer-Lytton: *Richelieu*

'The need for conservation of our natural resources, for the control of increasing pollution, to provide for a rapidly expanding population and to provide transportation systems to move the people about are all with us *now*.'

Lest you were under the impression that the self-regulation of population size, the capacity to behave selflessly, the technological fix-it, and the rest of them, constituted an exhaustive list of our self-deceptions, we shall quickly proceed to analyse a few more. The quotation above is taken from a document entitled *Report on proceedings of the seminar held at Monash University on 26 February, 1972 on the Board of Works report 'Planning Policies for the Melbourne Metropolitan Region'*.[1] The writer is no less imposing than the title: His Excellency, Major General Sir Rohan Delacombe, Governor of Victoria.

Now it would be quite unjustifiable to criticize Sir Rohan; the little delusion that he is expressing is a widespread one with some very respectable adherents. Their most eloquent spokesman is unquestionably Barry Commoner of Washington University, the man (a publisher's blurb informs me) whom *Time* magazine has called 'the Paul Revere of ecology'.

The following words *do not* occur in the index of one of

Barry Commoner's books which I have in front of me: Birth Control, Contraception, Food Shortage, Overpopulation, Population Density, Population Growth, Starvation. And yet the book was printed in 1971, and it is called *Science and Survival*;[2] Chapter 7 is titled *To Survive on Earth*. It discusses pollution, resource depletion, nuclear war and social responsibility. But the real philosophy of the book is revealed by the title of Chapter 1, which is *Is Science Getting Out of Hand?*

Commoner, in fact, does not believe that population growth is an important part of the story of our demise. In his 1971 *The Closing Circle*[3] he wrote: 'despite the frequent assertions that blame the environmental crisis on "overpopulation", "affluence", or both, we must seek elsewhere for an explanation'. More specifically, he wrote in 1972:[4]

'In the period 1946–68 US population increased, at an approximately constant rate, by about 42 per cent; GNP (adjusted to 1958 dollars) increased exponentially by about 126 per cent; GNP [per head] also increased approximately exponentially by about 59 per cent.

We can see at once that, as a first approximation, the contribution of population growth to the overall values of the environmental impacts generated since 1946 is of the order of 40 per cent. In most cases, this represents a relatively small contribution to the environmental impact, since . . . these values increased by 200 – 2000 per cent during the period. '

The gist of the argument is, then, that resource consumption and environmental destruction are growing much faster than is population; that we should therefore concentrate our energy on *them*, and worry less about controlling population, which, in an industrialized country, is a 'relatively small' factor. This, of course, is exactly the view that Sir Rohan Delacombe is expressing: he believes that it is possible simultaneously to *increase* population, *increase* resource conservation, and *decrease* pollution. It's just a slightly elaborated version of the 'greatest good of the greatest number' principle.

Now no one, I am sure, is denying that pollution and environmental degradation are truly monumental horrors, and that we should be busting ourselves in an effort to halt them. But to assert that we can do anything effective about them unless we simultaneously tackle population control is demonstrably false. Solving these problems is necessary, certainly, but it is far from sufficient. It would be a clear case of the little Dutch boy sticking his finger in a minute hole in the dyke while a few yards away a torrent of water poured in through a breach four feet in diameter.

Here is what another adherent of the Commoner doctrine, A. J. Coale[5] of Princeton University, has to say about population:

'It seems to me that malnutrition usually accompanies poverty and ignorance; moreover, poverty and ignorance exist, and have long existed, in many societies, whatever the size of the population . . . I suppose one could argue that *any* area where there is poverty and ignorance is overpopulated, but this form of circular reasoning is scarcely helpful in achieving a better understanding or in formulating a sensible policy. A similar point could be made (perhaps with less force) about environmental deterioration and endangered ecosystems . . . I have pointed out before that pollution of the air and water is a serious problem in parts of Australia.'

Since these words were written in a critique of the Ehr-

lichs' *Population, Resources, Environment*,[6] we should perhaps let Paul Ehrlich answer for himself, as he did in *Science*,
March 1971.[7] To summarize his arguments briefly here: he
points out that population growth has a *disproportionate*
environmental impact. Thus one per cent population growth
results in far more than a one per cent increase in environmental degradation. Consider the very simplest of examples:
a population where every person has links (roads, telephone
lines, etc., all of them involving land alienation and resource
consumption) with every other person. This is how the series
goes: 1 person, 0 links, 2 people, 1 link; 3 people, 3 links; 4
people, 6 links; 5 people, 10 links; 6 people, 15 links . . . 100
people, 4,950 links; 200 people, 19,900 links. Now compare
those last two sets of figures. Population has doubled: a 100
per cent increase. The number of links, on the other hand,
has increased by just over 300 per cent. Are we to say that
population growth accounts for only one third of this increase?

The other major consideration is the problem of diminish-
ing returns. Consider minerals or petroleum:

> 'As the richest supplies of these resources and those
> nearest to centres of use are consumed, we are obliged to
> use lower-grade ores, drill deeper, and extend our supply
> networks. All these activities increase our . . . use of energy
> and our . . . impact on the environment . . . Diminishing
> returns are also operative in increasing food production to
> meet the needs of growing populations. Typically, attempts
> are made both to overproduce on land already farmed and
> to extend agriculture to marginal land. The former requires
> disproportionate energy use in obtaining and distributing
> water, fertilizers and pesticides. The latter also increases
> . . . energy use, since the amount of energy invested per
> unit yield increases as less desirable land is cultivated.'[7]

'There are three kinds of lies,' said Disraeli, 'Lies, damned lies and statistics,' and in essence Commoner and Coale are using statistics to tailor the truth more than somewhat. Since 1940, Coale notes, aluminium consumption in the US has increased by over 1400 per cent, while in the same period the US population has increased by only (*only?*) 50 per cent. True, of course; but much of the increase in aluminium consumption has been because it has increasingly been used to replace steel; combined consumption of aluminium *and* steel has grown by only 117 per cent since 1940.[7] An even blunter statistical instrument is shown in what we may call the 'Australia fallacy'. Australia is grossly underpopulated compared to, say, the United Kingdom (population densities: UK, 1.4 persons per acre; Australia, 1 person per 150 acres), and yet, as Coale rightly remarks, Australia has air and water pollution problems. But overall population density is a meaningless statistic to use in this context: the air and water pollution problems are most serious in some very restricted areas of Australia, which go by the names of Sydney, Melbourne, Adelaide, and so on. The population density of Melbourne is 1.7 persons to the acre. If by population density we mean the density at which people live, then for most Australians their population density is very high, since more than two-thirds of them live in the big cities. I rather doubt whether John Melbourne and Fred Sydney are very interested in the fact that there is relatively little air pollution in the middle of the Simpson Desert.

This is a logical point at which to dispose, in passing, of another of our fondest delusions: decentralization. Decentralization is a process which presupposes increasing population, increasing production and consumption, increasing pollution, increasing habitat destruction; from those points of view alone it is clearly the last thing we want. But if you are stuck with a growing population surely it's better to house it away from the present centres of density? Certainly: it takes the pressure off; it lets people hide from the immediacy of the problem of urban disintegration. It ensures that in the long term the whole problem is going to become *worse*. There is a very simple factor which governs the location people choose to reside in: they live where they want to. So some of your grand new cities will grow into dirty old ones, and people will start to talk about decentralization all over again; others will remain little bitty cities because, no matter what you do, people won't want to live in them. By housing half a million people in a new city instead of tacking them on to the edge of an old one you are, first and foremost, ensuring that the impact of this additional population is quite disproportionate to its size. Your new city will naturally be located on good, fertile, pleasant land (isn't it a funny coincidence how man seems to prefer living in the sorts of places and climates where his food grows best?); so for a start you will have destroyed thousands of acres of potentially productive land. Secondly, resource consumption will be massive: all those new facilities you have to provide – airports, highways, hospitals, schools, printing presses . . . And thirdly, wherever you house those people, new city or old, it is not going to help one damn bit in the alleviation of the most serious of our survival crises: resource depletion, global pollution (such as carbon dioxide production), population growth and so on. Rather it will ensure that these processes are accelerated beyond their present breakneck speed.

I accept completely the proposition that, given stable populations, rational resource consumption, control of pollution, and all the rest of it, it would be a good idea to decrease the size of our largest cities. But we are not given any of that; and decentralization is in consequence an irrelevancy, an excursion into futility. The whole question is largely academic in any case, because whether you believe decentralization to be good or bad in theory does not alter the fact that, in practice, it barely exists. Decentralization has been a political catch-cry in Australia since the year dot; in spite of this, population growth of the state capitals has been outstripping population growth of the states by a bigger margin each year. These are the figures for Adelaide: in 1901 it contained 45.4% of South Australia's population; in 1921, 51.6%; in 1947, 59.2%; in 1966, 66.6%.[6]

Let us again allow Paul Ehrlich[7] a word on the subject:

> 'People live where they do, not because of a perverse intention to add to the problems of their society but for reasons of economic necessity, convenience and desire for agreeable surroundings. Areas that are uninhabited or sparsely populated today are presumably that way because they are deficient in some of the requisite factors. In many cases, the remedy for such deficiencies – for example, the provision of water and power to the wastelands of central Nevada – would be extraordinarily expensive in dollars, energy and resources, and would probably create environmental havoc.'

Granted all that, I nevertheless begin to wonder at this point whether the decentralizers, the Coales, the Commoners, do not perhaps have much greater insight than I am giving them credit for. It may well be that they have decided to concentrate their energies on the pollution bomb because they see some faint hope of defusing it; perhaps they have already arrived at the conclusion which most of us still refuse to accept: that that other bomb, the population one, is impossible to defuse. It is now clear that deliberate birth control, as a possibility for limiting population size, has resoundingly taken its place on our honour roll of Grand Delusions. This is of course self-evident, from the facts we have outlined regarding man's biological nature, if for no other reason; we do not need to go into those arguments again. We noted that birth control has always been widely practised by man; practised as a means of increasing population growth. There is no evidence to suggest that it has ever been used as a mechanism for decreasing it; nor, in terms of natural selection theory, would we expect to find such evidence. The possibility of deliberately reducing reproductive success, reducing fitness, has no precedent; like prudential restraint, it as an evolutionary *non sequitur*.

It is inevitable, therefore, that the question, 'Has there ever been a successful, deliberate, self-imposed population control programme?' is virtually a rhetorical one. The answer is of course *no*, never, not anywhere. Remember that we are not talking about the lowering of a population growth rate from 2% to 1% or whatever – though that is a truly remarkable achievement. On the other hand where it has happened it has been in a way we do not understand, and through no conscious efforts of our own. We are talking about the necessity for growth rates to become 0% or to become negative; present populations of many countries are too large for them to be viable in the long, or even medium, term.

The country that immediately comes to mind at this point is, of course, Japan. Japan, it is perfectly true, decreased its birth rate substantially after the Second World War, from 35/1,000 in 1945 to 18/1,000 in 1957, thereby halving its growth rate, from 2% to 1%.[9] This was very largely achieved, incidentally, through the medium of abortion: in 1949 there were a quarter of a million legal abortions in Japan; in 1955, one and a quarter million.

We need note only two things about the Japanese experience. *One*, that even in a highly industrialized, literate, 'civilized' country such as Japan, a birth control 'programme' which, we are told, had both popular support and government backing,, could do no better than lower the growth rate to 1%. 1%: that is the addition of *one million* people each year. That is a doubling time of seventy years; if you lived out your three score and ten there would be twice as many people on the day you died as on the day you were born. And *Two*, even this minor triumph has vanished into thin air. In *Science*, 13 February 1970, P. M. Boffey[10] notes that 'Japan is the most crowded nation in the world . . . the congestion seems unbelievable to many Westerners. Last summer . . . Prime Minister Eisaku Sato publicly advocated an *increase* in Japan's birthrate . . . The recommendation is aimed at alleviating some potentially serious economic and social problems . . . One such problem is a worsening labour shortage that threatens to undermine Japan's "economic miracle" . . .'

(Boffey also quotes a revealing statement by Toshio Kuroda of the government's Institute for Population Problems, concerning the postwar decline in Japan's birthrate: 'The government had no definite policy to bring about population control. It just happened under the very extraordinary situation after the war. Ten years later people looked back and said we were successful at controlling our population. But no expert in Japan predicted it would happen.')

At any rate Mr Sato can survey the scene from his retirement with a great deal of satisfaction. By the end of 1970 Japan had taken his words to heart so enthusiastically that its population was 'growing as fast as or faster than the US, the USSR, and all the major nations of Europe except Rumania'.[11]

It could be argued that Japan, being prosperous, well-fed, and enjoying a high standard of living (apart from smog, mercury poisoning, and the like), has no real incentive for applying birth control measures. The true test may rather be an undeveloped country where malnutrition and starvation are already rampant. In this case we must of course look at India, the first country in Asia to launch a birth control programme. This occurred in 1952, when India's birth rate was 40/1,000. In 1970 – after eighteen years of attempted control – the birth rate was 42/1,000. In the same period the death rate declined from 27/1,000 to 17/1,000, so that a 1952 growth rate of 1.3% became one of 2.5%. Thus if asked the question, 'What has been the major demographic trend in India since a birth control programme was instituted in 1952?', one would be obliged to answer, 'The population growth rate has very nearly doubled.'

Of course it is easy to rationalize this disastrous defeat. Thus W. D. Borrie[12] writes:

'There is a tendency for many to assume that birth control is anathema to, or impossible to achieve amongst, the semi-literate masses of Asian peasantry. The absence of positive results from India . . . is often cited as evidence to support these conclusions. In fact, given the complexity and magnitude of the task confronting these countries, as well as the half century of time which it took most of today's developed nations to achieve the demographic transition from high to low fertility, it would be indeed surprising if there were yet many visible signs of success in such efforts, for they are for the most part not much more than a decade old.'

Now apart from the obvious red herrings in this statement (e.g. reference to the demographic transition, which, as we have mentioned, has occurred only in industrialized countries; the description of such countries as India, Pakistan, Laos and Malaysia as 'semi-literate' when UN figures reveal adult literacy rates of 30% or less; and use of the phrase *visible* signs – implying that there are probably all sorts of *invisible* ones), I would ask you to apply a simple test to its implications. Suppose the figures we have quoted referred not to Indian birth rates but to road casualties in your nation. If your government announced new safety laws which had the stated aim of reducing a 1952 road toll of 40/1,000 to 30/1,000 by 1970 (India's aim was to reduce births to 25/1,000 by 1973); and the actual toll in 1970 was 42/1,000, would you murmur about 'visible signs' and 'scarcely more than a decade'? Or would you say, 'Hell, this is patently absurd – whoever designed these new laws needs his head read'?

Let me quote rather more realistically from Dr S. Israel,[13] Officer-in-Charge of the Bombay Family Planning Training and Research Centre:

'. . . in spite of the intense educational and motivational programmes carried out and despite the integration of family planning with many other welfare services (1) there is no impact on the general birth rate . . . and (2) there is continued lack of interest in the use of contraceptives on the part of the majority of couples . . . Vigorous measures must continue for raising the general level of education of the people, for securing a high standard of living and for creating in the general population a firm conviction that family planning is an essential means for maintaining this standard. And for this sort of programme time and extensive resources of finance and skilled manpower are imperative.'

So these are what India needs: good education, a high standard of living, an excellent system of communications, large numbers of skilled personnel, a considerable amount of time and a hell of a lot of money. Just what are the chances of India getting one, never mind all, of those things?

The whole history of attempts at deliberate birth control has been illustrative of another of our most commonly-employed self-deceptions: what we may call the *If only* syndrome. *If only* people were better educated, they would co-operate with birth control programmes. So we should start by educating them. *If only* we had the perfect contraceptive . . . How much more perfect can a contraceptive be? How come swallowing a pill is an acceptable – even venerated – solution to most of our other problems, but it *isn't* an ideal form of birth control? Sooner or later we shall presumably realize that there is really just one *If only* that matters: If only deliberate birth control were possible, we would be able to impose deliberate birth control.

And then there is that other little quirk of human nature which has had unfortunate consequences for our faith in birth control programmes. Suppose you are put in charge of a birth control clinic in India, or Bangladesh, or Colombia; at the end of your first year of operations your superior officer calls you into his room and says, 'Well, what have you achieved?' What the hell can you tell him? Nothing, really, so you have to say something like: 'Oh, great progress, sir! We've distributed three quarters of a million free condoms and two hundred thousand free IUDs; we've held a hundred and ten screenings of birth control films; we've distributed fifty thousand leaflets containing sterilization propaganda; we've given lectures in seventy-nine villages . . .' Good answer, you see: full of statistics, full of evidence of what a hard-working chap you are. And even better, it's an answer for all seasons; it'll do just as well ten years later if you bung in a few more millions and hundred thousands here and there. You're naturally not going to admit that you have nothing positive to say, and he doesn't want to be told that the programme his government has invested millions of dollars in is a fizz. So everyone is happy, and the only really vital question – how many births have *not* occurred that *would have* occurred in the absence of this programme? – need never be asked or answered.

The whole trouble with birth control is that it is just that: birth *control*. It cuts right across the most sacred of our many sacred cows – it is an 'infringement of personal liberty', it is 'contrary to the laws of nature', it is 'denying God's plan for mankind'. And it also has a nasty, legislative, bureaucratic ring about it; let's rather call it *family planning*, following the identical ritual by which we call airsickness *motion discomfort*, secondhand cars *pre-owned cars*, and – glorious legacy of Watergate! – barefaced lies *inoperative statements*. Oh yes, our government spent x million dollars on family planning last year; you can see we're taking this business seriously. Good work, you say; but remember that family planning need have very little to do with birth control. Family planning is essentially having as many children as you want but timing, or planning, when they arrive. So an unplanned family may consist of four children born at yearly intervals; a planned family of four children born at intervals of one, three, and one years. (A closely similar technique is used in handling questions about pollution: 'Air pollution, did you say? Let me tell you that this government invested *twelve million dollars* in air pollution monitoring programmes last year. Don't you worry – we've got the situation well in hand.' And what does *monitoring* mean? *Watching*, that's what: 'We're not letting all this air pollution happen unnoticed, you know. We're *watching* it happen. We're not letting the biosphere fall apart all by itself – no fear – we're carefully and conscientiously *watching* it fall apart.')

Let us conclude this section with a quote from another of today's biological giants, J. Z. Young.[14] This was written in 1971, and you may like to judge for yourself how fairly it summarizes the present state of the art:

'With the coming of improved and simpler methods it seems likely that contraception will spread widely and perhaps rapidly, as it has in Japan, Taiwan and India. Programmes or policies for population control exist in many countries and the list grows longer every year. Of countries with populations over 25 million only Nigeria, Brazil and Burma have no such policies. Of course to have a population control policy does not mean the actual reduction in rate of growth of population, which has been achieved in Japan, Hong Kong, Singapore, and perhaps S. Korea. The great numbers of young men and women in the countries with "young" populations will certainly produce a greatly increased population in the next few years. It is unlikely that the "population explosion" will continue along precisely the same lines shown by the curves of even the recent past. Many people already know how to limit their families and more and more will soon know. It is probable that contraception will become much more general, but no one knows just what effect this will have on population numbers.'

My only comment is that those eight sentences contain the phrases *it seems likely*, *perhaps* (twice), *it is unlikely*, *it is probable*, and *no one knows*; and that's as good a reason as any for abandoning this topic.

We can deal fairly briefly with three more lights that failed, because their failure has already been well documented. The first of them, the possibility that we shall be able to produce vastly increased quantities of food in the near future, is unusual in that we have here reversed our usual self-delusory technique. Normally we hitch our wagons to a fallacy – birth control, space travel, or whatever – and declare our undying faith in it. But in the present case we have identified what we consider to be a fallacy and busily set out to *prove* that it is one. Needless to say, what we have labelled 'the Malthusian fallacy' is no more nor less than the plain and simple truth; in this instance the fallacy is to think it *is* a fallacy.

'One may reasonably argue,' writes W. D. Borrie[12], 'that just as Malthus failed to appreciate the effects of technology and the opening up of new lands upon carrying capacity, so many of today's environmentalists and technologists may not take sufficient account either of future technological advance, or of the application of the newer biological and genetical sciences to create a "green revolution" in the area of food production.' More dogmatically, Robert Ardrey[15] tells us that 'there is sufficient evidence . . . to warrant the conclusion that Malthus was wrong'. And the whizziest kid of them all, R. Buckminster Fuller[16] writes: 'Humanity's mastery of vast, inanimate, inexhaustible energy sources and the accelerated doing more with less of sea, air and space technology has proven Malthus to be wrong.'

Malthus *was* wrong in many details; the actual times that he put on some of his forecasts, for instance, were hopelessly out. And, as Borrie says, he could not have foreseen the opening up of the New World, nor the green revolution. But the fact remains that what he said was this:

> 'The power of population is indefinitely greater than the power in the earth to produce subsistence for man. Population, when unchecked, increases in a geometrical ratio. Subsistence increases only in an arithmetical ratio.* A

* A geometrical ratio is the exponential progression we have already come across: 1, 2, 4, 8, 16, 32, 64 . . . An arithmetical ratio (or progression) is described by 1, 2, 3, 4, 5, 6, 7 . . .

slight acquaintance with numbers will shew the immensity of the first power in comparison of the second.

By that law of nature which makes food necessary to the life of man, the effects of these two unequal powers must be kept equal. This implies a strong and constantly operating check on population from the difficulty of subsistence. This difficulty must fall somewhere and must necessarily be severely felt by a large portion of mankind.'[17]

And that, in general terms, is a good description of the situation facing us today. 'Malthus' fears may at last be irremediably confirmed,' wrote Joseph Spengler[18] in 1969. 'Within little more than a century the world's population may have grown abreast of the world's food supply of that time . . .' (But that *little more than a century* doesn't sound too bad, does it?)

I do not think we need to involve ourselves in protracted discussion of the Green Revolution. This rather grandiose name refers to the development and widespread adoption of new varieties of rice and wheat; and no one can doubt that the resulting increases in yield have been spectacular. US Department of Agriculture[19] figures show, for example, that wheat production per head of population in India increased by 43 per cent between 1960 and 1968; in Pakistan by 33 per cent; cereal production per person in Mexico increased by 38 per cent in the same period. The fact that we now have the potential to achieve enormous increases in food production is not in dispute. The question really is whether or not this means that we can stop worrying about population growth; and it is now clear that the answer is firmly in the negative. For a start, the above figures, impressive as they are, are rapidly cut back to size when they are set against the needs they are supposed to meet. The Food and Agriculture Organization of the UN estimates that between now and the end of the century, to provide a *minimum* diet for the peoples of Africa, Latin America, and the Far East, the food supplies of these areas will have to increase by 160%, 240% and 300%, respectively. Let's next take a quote from Lester Brown,[19] former Administrator of the International Agricultural Development Service of the US Department of Agriculture. In 1971 he wrote: 'The Green Revolution is clearly not a solution to the food-population problem, but it is buying time with which to stabilize population growth.' There is also a newspaper record of a 'debate' between Norman Borlaug, who received a Nobel Prize for his development of high-yield Mexican wheat, and Georg Borgstrom, Professor of Food Science at the University of Michigan. With typical frivolity Borlaug is labelled an 'optimist' by the newspaper, Borgstrom a 'pessimist' (as regards the world food situation). Here are a few quotes from the article:[20]

Borlaug: The green revolution is not a uniform thing, and progress is still very small compared with the total need . . . And it can buy only a very little time in which to adjust population growth to reasonable levels.

Borgstrom: I think there is a reasonable chance of managing [to sustain the green revolution] for the rest of the century. But that is on one assumption: that we move to strict population control now, in the 1970s.

Borlaug: I wouldn't disagree.

[*Who is the optimist? Here is what they think about the world's water supply:*]

Borgstrom: Because of water shortage, mankind is *now* only one or two years from starvation . . .

Borlaug: This is just what I've been trying to say for the past few years. In general, I'd agree that water is very critical . . .

[*And on another of our dreams, food from the sea:*]

Borgstrom: The claims have been very exaggerated. The oceans look vast, but we forget they contain large desert areas . . .
Borlaug: I agree absolutely . . .

In Lester Brown's[19] summary of the world food situation he predicts that the catch of fish per person will *decline* by the end of the century. He notes that the following fisheries have already declined: Antarctic blue whale, East African sardine, Northwest Pacific salmon, Atlantic herring, Barents Sea cod, and Antarctic fin whale. Fisheries on the verge of decline (in that increased effort is no longer bringing increased yield) include tuna and menhaden in all the major oceans; herring, cod, perch, flounder and hake in the North Atlantic; anchovy in the South Eastern Pacific; and plaice and haddock in the North and Barents Seas. He further points out that man's dreams of 'farming' the oceans have no imminent hope of becoming reality, and that our only chance for the immediate future is to increase yields on land.

Perhaps we can also allow Lester Brown[19] the last word on the subject of food in general:

'Various estimates have been made of how many people the earth can feed. Some of these estimates are several times the current population size. It is now becoming increasingly clear that those making the estimates have been asking the wrong question. The question is not, How many people can the earth feed? but, What are the environmental and social consequences of attempting to feed so many? . . . In the light of what we now know, there is growing doubt that the earth's agricultural ecosystem can support the 6.5 billion* people projected for the year 2000. The growing evidence argues strongly for the stabili-

* American usage (a thousand million).

zation of global population growth well before the end of this century.'

(As Norman Borlaug said elsewhere in the interview quoted earlier, 'We always come back to this population thing'.)

Thomas Malthus, however right or wrong you judge him to be on the general issue of food versus population, had indisputably clear vision on one point: the contribution that migration of peoples could make to the solution of food shortage problems. In his *A Summary View of the Principle of Population* (1830)[21] he wrote:

'Whatever temporary and partial relief, therefore, may be derived from emigration by particular countries in the actual state of things, it is quite obvious that, considering the subject generally and largely, emigration may be fairly said not in any degree to touch the difficulty. And whether we exclude or include emigration – whether we refer to particular countries, or to the whole earth – the supposition of a future capacity in the soil to increase the necessaries of life every twenty-five years by a quantity equal to that which is at present produced must be decidedly beyond the truth.'

He had a lucid vision of what we now call the 'Spaceship Earth' concept: moving people around *within* the spaceship makes no difference to the amount of food they require. And the economic difficulties of large-scale migration have been clearly understood for years: George Kuriyan[22] noted in 1962 that emigration was strictly a non-answer to India's population problem. To really do any good, he said, you would have to move out about a third of India's population (150 million people when he wrote; 195 million when I was writing the first rough draft of this manuscript; and more like 205 million now). And you would need to do this 'in the twinkle of an eye'; if emigration were slow, reproduction would make up the loss. Merely to keep up with natural increase you would have to export about 15 million people a year. Where would you send them – to the wide open spaces of Australia? One year's export would more than double Australia's population, a prospect which would probably delight the Australian government but for the headaches it would mean in terms of houses, schools, hospitals, food, etc.

All this is completely obvious and we don't need to labour the point. But it does make an interesting background to a little furore that occurred in Australia in April 1972, and it in turn is nicely illustrative of how hard our old wives' tales die.

On 24 April 1972 Sir Philip Baxter, one-time chairman of the Australian Atomic Energy Commission, was interviewed on television. Primarily he was being asked about Australia's energy needs in the future and how they were to be met, but the more general issues of population, resources, environment, inevitably arose. Sir Philip, with a sort of matter-of-fact air of explaining the obvious, pointed out that a global disaster was inevitable around or before the turn of the century. Nuclear war, epidemic disease or famine were the possibilities he envisaged. He went on to say that Australia would have a better chance than most nations of surviving such a catastrophe, being a relatively lightly-populated, isolated, southern-hemisphere island. So far, so good – that's the sort of thing that people like to hear. But then he added that in these circumstances Australia would be a 'lifeboat' for the world, with hordes of homeless, starving refugees trying to climb aboard. Australia, he said, should provide itself with bacteriological, chemical or nuclear weapons, or 'anything else which will enable one man to hold off a hundred'. It should be getting ready now to make sure it has the means to repel these boarders when they arrive.

Pandemonium! 'Barbaric', said the President of the Australian Council of Churches; 'immoral and selfish' was the view of the Roman Catholic Archbishop of Melbourne. 'Un-Christian and unacceptable', thundered the Democratic Labour Party; while the Australian Labour Party contented itself with 'unworthy of comment . . . hard to understand'. The President of the Victorian Society for Social Responsibility in Science, on the other hand, expressed his belief that 'the world would be responsible enough never to let the sort of situation that Sir Philip envisages ever eventuate'.

Of course the newspapers had a field day too. *The Age*,[28] in its editorial of 26 April, said:

'As an expression of considered thought and a brief for possible government action, Sir Philip's remarks are contemptible. The fact that they come from a man who until recently held the important post of chairman of the Australian Atomic Energy Commission is disturbing . . . Sir Philip's lurid picture of Australia using nuclear rockets to shoot down or sink ship loads or Jumbo-jet loads of refugees from the northern hemisphere has a cold and conscienceless quality about it. A nation that had to base its future policies on such inhuman and despairing notions would be in the final stages of moral decay. Australia has not sunk so low and, pray God, never will.'

On the same day *The Age*'s public affairs columnist plaintively headed his piece 'Solutions please, no scares'. Among other things, he wrote:

'The overwhelming need in Australia is to shed the kind of hair-brained (sic) realism that has from our beginnings governed our attitude to the rest of the world. We need less cataclysmic futurology and more practical advice, especially from our scientists, on how we can contribute to a manageable world.'

Poor Sir Philip . . . he committed the ultimate crime; he trespassed against the eleventh commandment: *Thou shalt not face reality, nor ask others to face it*. But amongst all the tumult and the shouting a few points got by without comment. First, who of all the critics suggested an alternative to what Sir Philip was advocating? Nobody. Second, how do his ideas line up with Australia's *present* policies on immigration? Pretty well, really. Of course Australia doesn't drop bombs on immigrants, because it has no need to – yet – but it is damned careful to regulate minutely who, and how many, come in. Australia is at present a well-fed island in an overwhelmingly undernourished world; does it let the starving hordes in? Of course not. Australia will be, says Sir Philip, a well-fed island in an even more undernourished world; will it, in that situation, do an abrupt about-face and unlock the gates? And suppose the crowds outside the gates are beating on them with battering rams: will Australia say, 'Now, now, chaps . . . a few of you can come in but the rest will have to run along home', and expect to achieve anything?

But we should not expect questions like these to be asked or answered. Sir Philip tried to make us think the unthinkable, face the unfaceable; and it is our duty to point out to him the error of his ways. There are all sorts of things he's overlooked . . . the world would be responsible enough never to let it happen, just as it used and is using its great responsibility at Hiroshima, at Auschwitz, at Sharpeville, in Biafra, in the Middle East, in South East Asia. He's being immoral, selfish, un-Christian, and therefore he's wrong; immoral, un-Christian things just don't happen: selfishness is simply unheard of. And he should be thinking positively about 'practical advice' rather than spouting all this 'cataclysmic futurology'; all he has to do is draw on our great storehouse of scientific wizardry and he'll see everything much more clearly.

Perhaps we might borrow Sir Philip's lifeboat analogy to illustrate another of the fixes which the world refuses to acknowledge that it's in. There you are in a lifeboat, four of you, way off the shipping lanes, hundreds of miles from land; and you have only a quart of drinking water. What do you do? Do you say, 'Right, chaps: there's half a pint each; let's drink it up – something is sure to turn up tomorrow'? Or do you ration it out, mouthful by mouthful, sip by sip, for as long as you possibly can?

The world is the lifeboat, and the drinking water is the world's resources. We have, needless to say, chosen the first of the two alternative courses of action.

We don't need to elaborate greatly on this theme. Both petroleum and natural gas will be virtually exhausted within the lifetimes of people alive today; are we doing our damnedest to limit their use only to the most essential of purposes? By the year 2000 chances are we shall have also run out of lead, zinc, tin, mercury, gold, silver, platinum and uranium-235 (to name a few); has that affected our usage of these metals? Naturally not; *something* will turn up to save the day. The technological fix, the extraction of minerals from sea water, the substitution of one mineral for another; we have all sorts of cards up our sleeves. We can similarly handle the problems of water shortage and energy shortage; desalination, breeder reactors, solar energy . . . we have a pocketful of technological miracles.

There has never been any limit to man's technical achievement. He began as a fearful, furtive, ground-dwelling primate endowed with good eyesight, a large brain, and extraordinarily skilful hands; and there he might have stayed but for his mastery of his environment. He scrutinized it with those sharp eyes, summed it up with that cunning brain, and then bent it to his own ends with those restless fingers. He exists in his present form wholly and solely because of his ability to control virtually any aspect of his environment that he chooses. He *had* to; it was his key to survival, his road to the stars. The more completely he could control his habitat and turn it to his own purposes, the better was his survival assured. And so he went on, to greater and greater things. He became the first and only primate to build a roof over his head, to warm himself with fire, to fly in the air and sail on the sea, to go to the moon and to massacre millions of his fellows . . . There was no one who could stop him; there was no need for him to stop himself.

Was there never to be a limit? Of course, one reared its head now and then . . . but there was nearly always a way round it. If you ran out of land you moved on and discovered the New World. If your farm started to lose its sweetness you manufactured some fertilizer and spread it around. If you became sick you invented a medicine and were better again. If, and if, and if . . .

But there *are* limits. It's just that we have so rarely had to face them that we now refuse to acknowledge that they exist. The four-minute mile could never be run, but it was . . . but the two-minute mile will never be run. The moon had always been the paragon of unattainability until we reached it, but we shall never reach the stars. We can sustain 200 odd million people at the USA's standard of living, but we can never sustain 2,000 million. *Those* are the limits, and incredibly, impossibly, inconceivably, we have started to reach them.

The woods decay, the woods decay and fall,
The vapours weep their burden to the ground,
Man comes and tills the field and lies beneath,
And after many a summer dies the swan.

We have had nearly all our summers.

NOTES

1 MELBOURNE AND METROPOLITAN BOARD OF WORKS. *Report on proceedings of the seminar held at Monash University on 26 February, 1972 on the Board of Works report 'Planning Policies for the Melbourne Metropolitan Region'* (1972)

2 COMMONER, BARRY. *Science and Survival* (London, Gollancz, 1966)

3 COMMONER, BARRY. *The Closing Circle* (London, Jonathan Cape 1971)

4 COMMONER, BARRY. 'The environmental cost of economic growth', *Chemistry in Britain*, Vol. 8 (1972) 52-65

5 COALE, ANSLEY J. 'Disastrous Numbers', *Science*, Vol. 170 (1970) 428-29

6 EHRLICH, PAUL R., and EHRLICH, ANNE H. *Population, Resources, Environment* (Reading, W. H. Freeman 1970)

7 EHRLICH, PAUL R., and HOLDREN, JOHN P. 'Impact of Population Growth', *Science*, Vol. 171 (1971) 1212-17

8 WILLIAMS, MICHAEL (ed.). *South Australia from the Air* (Melbourne University Press 1969)

9 WILSON, M. G. A. *Population Geography* (London, Thomas Nelson 1968)

10 BOFFEY, P. M. 'Japan: A Crowded Nation Wants to Boost Its Birthrate', *Science*, Vol. 167 (1970) 960-62

11 EHRLICH, PAUL R., and HARRIMAN, RICHARD L. *How to be a Survivor* (Ballantine Books 1971)

12 BORRIE, W. D. 'The Population Factor', *Search*, Vol. 2 (1970) 363-68

13 ISRAEL, S. Quoted by WILSON, M. G. A. *Population Geography* (London, Thomas Nelson 1968)

14 YOUNG, J. Z. *An Introduction to the Study of Man* (Oxford University Press 1971)

15 ARDREY, ROBERT. *The Social Contract* (London, Collins 1970)

16 FULLER, R. BUCKMINSTER. Quoted by D. H. MEADOWS, D. L. MEADOWS, J. RANDERS and W. W. BEHRENS. 1972. *The Limits to Growth* (London, Earth Island 1972)

17 MALTHUS, THOMAS. *An Essay on the Principle of Population* (1798)

18 SPENGLER, JOSEPH J. 'Population Problem: In Search of a Solution', *Science*, Vol. 166 (1969) 1234-38

19 BROWN, LESTER, and FINSTERBUSCH, GAIL. 'Man, Food and Environment', in: William W. Murdoch (ed.), *Environment: Resources, Pollution and Society* (Sinauer Associates 1971)

20 THE AGE, MELBOURNE (18 March 1972)

21 MALTHUS, THOMAS. *A Summary View of the Principle of Population* (1830)

22 KURIYAN, GEORGE. 'Migration as a Solution', in: Garrett Hardin (ed.), *Population, Evolution and Birth Control.* (Reading, W. H. Freeman 1969)

23 THE AGE, MELBOURNE (26 April 1972)

8 Doing the Logical Thing

'Diseases desperate grown by desperate appliance are relieved, or not at all.'

Shakespeare: *Hamlet*

Crisis in the railways! We made a loss of 13.4 million dollars last year, gentlemen; and we simply can't afford to let this sort of thing continue. Our accountants inform me that if we increase fares by a mere 2.5 per cent this will enable us to reduce the deficit by . . . (*One year later*) – Our loss last year, I regret to say, gentlemen, was 18.7 million dollars. It is estimated that the fare increase drove away something of the order of 400,000 passengers. I think, with the advantage of hindsight, we can say that increasing fares was in fact *the precise opposite* of the course we should have taken . . .

Crisis in the boardroom! Our production figures, as you can see, sir, have grown far less rapidly than we expected. Now I've identified the hold-up on the line: the machinists *here*, you see, get their material from this conveyor *here*, and from each batch they can cut nine spangle-binders; then they have to go back for another lot. Now what I'm suggesting is that we simply enlarge the batches, so that each will provide material for fifteen rather than nine units. Time lost will thus be reduced by approximately . . . (*Next year*) – I'm sorry to say, sir, that our new production schedules have not really achieved the success we'd hoped for. I did of course commission a closer analysis, and I think I've found the weak spot: the nine-unit batches were, it seems, about the biggest that a machinist could possibly handle . . . our mistake was to enlarge them when we should have reduced them. I'm afraid we've got to face it: the remedy we tried last year *just couldn't have been more wrong* . . .

Two scenarios with just one thing in common: in both cases the *actual* result of an attempt to improve the system was the precise opposite of the *desired* result. And the explanation in both cases is also the same: the people responsible for the modification simply didn't understand, didn't know enough about, the systems they were dealing with. In each case they *did the logical thing* – they intuitively identified what they considered to be the weaknesses in the system, and acted in good faith on that basis. Herein lies a moral.

Jay W. Forrester is a Professor of Management at the Massachusetts Institute of Technology. There he studies the dynamics of systems, a system (according to my dictionary) being 'an assemblage or combination of things or parts forming a complex or unitary whole'; dynamics is 'the science or principles of forces acting in any field'. Hence, system dynamics: the study of the forces acting on and in systems, making them behave in the ways they do. We have already looked at some system dynamics: passengers and trainfares, boardrooms and machinists; each of our scenarios described a system and each had its own dynamics.

But, you may be wondering, how does an M.I.T. professor come into all of this? The foul-ups in both our systems were due merely to superficial analysis; if things had been checked out properly in the first place any fool could have told them their 'cures' wouldn't work; it hardly needs a professor of management. Maybe so. But those were simple systems: what about when you get to complex ones? Let's look, say, at traffic flow at a city intersection: how can you speed it up? What sort of factors do you need to take into account? Well – the number of cars, obviously; and the direction they're going in, of course; and how long the peak periods last . . .

That should give you a pretty good idea. But will it? What about the effect of removing the traffic lights over there, because an overpass is being built? What effect will the closure of that factory have; and then there's this one which is going on to a three-shift system from next year? What about the combined influence of large crowds of football-goers travelling *this* way on Saturday evenings, while cinema-goers are heading *that* way? Have you taken into account the fact that on 23 per cent of winter evening peak periods it's drizzling or raining, which slows traffic by an average factor of 9 per cent? And were you aware that 62 per cent of housewives in this area are finished their shopping by 1610 hours in the winter, whereas in summer 56 per cent of them are still shopping at 1715 hours? How does that influence the system? And so it goes on.

Systems can become pretty complicated. Imagine trying to identify the dynamics governing the operation of a large corporation, or a government department, or a city. Imagine trying to answer questions like: Would it be better for us to employ one additional salesman in country areas or increase our TV advertising budget by 4 per cent? Or neither? Or what about: If this bridge can safely carry 0.29 thousand tons of traffic travelling in both directions on a dry, windless day when the temperature is 22°C; how many cars can it carry going in one direction at twice the speed on a rainy night with 40 knot winds and a temperature of −2°C?

It's these kinds of questions that need Jay Forresters to answer them. The more complex a system gets, the less competent we are at predicting its behaviour. A good illustration is our glorious system of capitalism and free enterprise. *Competition*, we said, and *choice*; they are what we need; they are what will result in healthy markets, in maintaining quality high and prices low. And what has happened in reality? – The exact opposite, of course: monopolies, takeovers, cartels, price-fixing; the obliteration of competition; the over-growth of corporations; and the consumer's champion Ralph Nader. Has it ever struck you that his very existence is an open confession of the failure of the whole dismal edifice?

Jay Forrester's system dynamics is a method of setting up a model – a computer analogue – of a system, and then examining the effects upon the system of changes to various of its components. The image that each of us has of his world is of course a model – a mental model – so there is nothing very revolutionary about the general idea. A computer model is simply a mental model generated through the correct programming of a computer. What is different about a computer model is that it can handle and examine far more intricate systems than can the human mind.

All systems, large or small, are finally reducible to a series of feedback loops; some positive, some negative. The loops in turn have two components: *levels* and *flow rates*. Your bank balance is a system. It has a *level*: the amount of money in it. It has *flows* of money in and out of it at various *rates*. The level is controlled by the flow rates; if, for a sustained period, more money goes out than comes in (i.e. the output flow rate is higher than the input one), the level falls. If the flow rates are the other way around, the level rises. The flow rates are also controlled by the level: if your account has only $30 in it you can't withdraw money at the rate of $10 a day for a week. The whole system consists of feedback loops: input is made up of interest (a positive feedback) and further deposits, which are controlled by how much money you earn or steal. Output is what you withdraw, and it is governed by your cost of living, and so on.

Jay Forrester and others like him began by constructing models, in these terms, of large corporations which were having problems: falling profits, high labour turnover, or whatever.[1] Often the company had itself tried to fix the problem, but with no success; the attempted remedy could, however, be simulated in the model. What turned out, time and time again, was that the corporation's supposed remedy was (*a*) having no effect; (*b*) worsening the problem; or (*c*) *causing* the problem. The system dynamics approach was then applied to cities,[2] and startlingly similar results emerged. Policies supposed to improve urban life were frequently making it worse.

Here's an example. You have a teeming, festering slum which you wish to get rid of: what do you do? Obviously, you demolish it. But what do you provide in its place? Again obviously: you must build high-density, low-cost accommodation. Reasoning: there are a hell of a lot of poor, over-crowded people in there so you have to give them cheap, abundant housing. This is the commonsense and universally accepted process of slum clearance.

But let us forget about common sense for a moment and scrutinize your reasoning. You've provided additional housing for low-income earners, so more of them come to the area. But you haven't provided additional jobs. So there is unemployment, which in turn leads to delinquency, to crime and vandalism . . . You have *lowered* the average income of the area; your nice new housing estate starts the downward slide. At some point, eventually, the area becomes so unattractive because of overcrowding, of crime, of broken windows and lifts that don't work, of a deplorable standard of living, that the inflow of people stops. And what do you have then? – a teeming, festering slum. So you build more high-density housing . . . 'If we were malicious and wanted to create urban slums, trap low-income people in ghetto areas and increase the number of people on welfare,' writes Forrester,[1] 'we could do little better than follow the present policies.'

Or take another case: you might have serious traffic congestion in peak hours. What are you going to do about it?

Clearly, build freeways . . . No more traffic congestion. But when all those cars get to the city they're going to have to park somewhere. OK, we thought of that: we're building a dozen multi-storey carparks. Great; now it's possible to get a parking spot more people bring their cars to the city. The freeways are starting to get a little congested . . . We'll build more. But then . . . We'll build more carparks, more freeways . . . You set out to relieve a traffic problem; you invest enormous amounts of time, money and energy; and the net result is to make the problem *worse*.

From examples like these Forrester[1] drew four important conclusions about the behaviour of social systems:

1. Social systems behave *counterintuitively*. That is, intuitive identifications of problems and obvious remedies are nearly always wrong; in fact they often make matters worse. The human mind is simply not equipped to understand, predict or control the activities of complex systems. The human brain, marvellous as it is, is unable to juggle with more than one or two levels and one or two flows over a period longer than one or two years. Nor should we expect it to. Cows evolved in the context of eating grass; we don't expect them to catch fish or play football. Lions evolved in the context of eating herbivores; we don't express astonishment because they can't graze on lucerne or fly to the moon. Man evolved in the context of small groups with immediate aims and policies; there is no earthly reason to expect him to be able to handle the intricacies of huge, diverse and complex groups over long periods of time. They represent a totally novel situation; one that he has never previously encountered in his evolutionary history; in turn there has never been any selective impetus in favour of those who could resolve such problems. Until trees evolved there was no conceivable virtue in having adaptations suitable for arboreal life; until complex social systems existed there was no point in having a

brain which could understand them.*

2. Social systems are characterized by conflict between the short-term and long-term consequences of policy changes. Short-term improvements nearly always result in long-term deterioration. It could be said, in fact, that ideal short-term solutions are also ideally suited to long-term degradation. We have looked at several examples of this kind of thing already. The converse is also generally true: remedies which are unpleasant and apparently having the wrong effect in the short term are often apt and effective in the long term.

3. Within a complex system there is conflict between the goals of individual sub-systems and the welfare of the system as a whole. If you try to maximize benefit in one area you will inevitably depress it in others. If you want high productivity and a high standard of living in your cities you can have them, but it will be at the expense of the country as a whole: pollution, environmental decay, resource depletion, and the rest of it. If your goal is to produce the greatest possible amount of food on the available land, you can, but in achieving this sub-system aim you have to do all kinds of mischief to the system as a whole.

4. Social systems are 'inherently insensitive to most policy changes that people select in an effort to alter behaviour. In fact, a social system draws attention to the very points at which an attempt to intervene will fail'.[2] We tend to apply our experience of simple systems (which our brain handles extremely well) to complex ones; we identify *immediate* causes and effects and are unable to recognize that they in

---

* Of course this general line of reasoning is not defensible in the absolute sense. The computer is, after all, a product of the human mind, and the human mind is in turn a product of the process of evolution; in this sense computer system dynamics is an evolutionary response to the challenge of understanding complex systems.

turn are parts of a larger system. Our attempts at pest control provide a good example: we reasoned, 'Lots of nasty bugs – spray poison – kill bugs – problem solved'. We *didn't*, until very recently, ask, '*Why* are there lots of nasty bugs?' We didn't realize that our methods of production – the elimination of diversity, monoculture, failure to rotate crops – were the cause of there being so many bugs in the first place. We identified and acted on a *proximate*, rather than an *ultimate*, cause-effect relationship. What drew our attention was the large number of bugs, and we acted on the simplistic assumption that killing them outright was the key to the problem.

Now you may well have come up with all sorts of objections to this analysis. With regard to the first characteristic, for instance, you may think, so what? We didn't ever fly through the air in heavier-than-air machines until just yesterday in our evolutionary history, either; but that hasn't stopped us from building – and flying – highly successful aeroplanes. Good point. But on the other hand we have to ask: Isn't flying just a logical extension of activity for a creature with a superb brain, excellent stereoscopic vision, good reflexes, exquisite balance, and all the rest of it? Flying didn't require the development of totally new capacities and skills; it just needed certain applications and combinations of the old ones. Further, the principle of flying is very simple, and we could make models and carry out tests before we committed ourselves. None of that is true of the analysis of social systems: it requires mental capacities that we simply don't have; we couldn't even begin to construct meaningful models until the advent of the electronic computer.

Again, you might be saying, Well, all right. Suppose this is all true. We now *have* the computers and the models so we *can* understand the systems and manage them properly: why need it be a problem any longer?

Let's go on to the next phase of Forrester's analysis; I

think the answer to that one will emerge of its own accord as we go along. In 1970 Jay Forrester attended a meeting of the Club of Rome, an international organization whose aims are to foster understanding, and hence promote new policies and effective actions, regarding what it calls the Predicament of Man. Since Forrester's system dynamics has proved so illuminating in the fields of corporation and urban management, it was suggested that he should, using the same methods, construct a model of that biggest social system of all, the world. And so he made a world model, which is described in some detail in his *World Dynamics*,[3] published in 1971.

The model is centred around five levels: population, capital investment, natural resources, fraction of capital devoted to agriculture, and pollution. The model starts at the year 1900, so that between 1900 and 1970 approximately real values for variables are used. What happens after 1970 depends on what you assume is going to happen to the various levels and flow rates. Three basic assumptions underlie the model: (*a*) that population and capital tend to grow exponentially; (*b*) that the earth is finite and therefore has a finite capacity for people, industries, waste, pollution, etc.; and (*c*) that there is delay in the operation of feedback processes which act to limit population and capital, hence 'overshoots' commonly occur, to be followed by 'crashes'.[4] Within this framework of not-very-radical assumptions you can generate any number of possible outcomes for the world as simulated in the model, depending on rates of population growth, resource usage, pollution build-up, and so on.

A diagram of the model appears on pages 20-21 of *World Dynamics*, and it is a fearsomely complicated looking thing. There are circles, rectangles, dots, dashes and arrows running riot everywhere. But it is not really as boggling as it at first seems. Take *Population*, for instance, one of the five levels in the system. It is affected by two major loops, Birth Rate and Death Rate. Each of these in turn is dependent on other factors: thus the birth rate varies with standard of living, availability of food, degree of crowding and seriousness of pollution; these things also affect the death rate. But pollution, say, is itself a function of population size and of standard of living; and standard of living is influenced by the amount of pollution. This is why you need a computer. In all, the model involves forty factors in addition to the five levels, so that with all the interrelationships, and mutual effects of these 45 variables on each other, it is not surprising that the diagram ends up looking something like a rather disorganized spider's web.

Nevertheless Forrester describes the model as 'preliminary', needing to be 'confirmed by more thorough research', and having implications which 'may well alter'. (In fact a refined version of the model has already appeared, in the Club of Rome endorsed *The Limits to Growth*.[5]) But at the same time we should remember that our models of the world up to now have been so rudimentary that they could barely even be described as 'preliminary'; nor have they been noticeably helpful. Forrester's one, constructed as it is, can hardly fail to be better. Obviously it is greatly oversimplified, but then our previous mental models were, by comparison, totally, ridiculously, oversimplified. It is also well to remember that, while our unaided mental models of *any* social system – corporation, city, planet – have been near-disasters, system dynamics has already proved its worth in the areas of corporation and urban management. Its world model comes to us with good credentials.

So what does one do with this splendid model? A reasonable analogy to its operation is provided by a planetarium, with which, by controlling the operation of the projector, one can construct a model of the night sky for any given date in the future. Of course the planetarium model is much simpler, because the stars are unwavering in their courses and we do not need very extensive data to tell us where they have been and where they are going. But the world model incorporates sufficient data to give us some idea of where *our* planet is going; a much harder thing to do. It can take into account virtually any combination of variables that might affect its future.

For a start, what does the world model predict if everything goes on much as it is: a world population growth rate of 2 per cent; food production and industrial output continuing to increase; and so on?

What it tells us to expect is that we shall run out of non-renewable resources. Population will continue to grow, requiring an ever-increasing input of resources; less can be invested for future growth. Finally industry will collapse, and with it will go agriculture, medical services, power generating systems, and so on. In turn will follow the deaths of hundreds of millions of people, from famine and the lack of health services. In the *World Dynamics* version of the model the population decline begins in about 2020, and by 2100 the population has decreased by 29 per cent.

But what if there are far greater quantities of resources than we now know of? Or what if Science finds ways to substitute other materials for what we now think are essential resources? The model handles both of those alternatives, and in either case its answer is the same. Starting in about 2000 there is a pollution crisis, and by 2060 pollution has risen to levels more than forty times higher than the present ones. Long before then population has plummeted, falling to less than 1,000 million by 2070. Hence Forrester,[1] in comparing this outcome to the natural resources depletion one, says '. . . we may not be fortunate enough to run gradually out of natural resources'.

Let's have another try. Say we manage to reduce the birth rate by 30 per cent or so in the next few years *and* cut resource consumption down to 25 per cent of its present level. What then? Population growth slows briefly, but as food availability improves the pressure is relaxed and it begins to climb again. As we might expect, there is again a pollution crisis, and population plunges just as it did before.

One last attempt. Let's assume we get natural resource use under control; also pollution, so that they are no longer threats. Also assume that crowding has no deleterious effects on humans: What will the outcome now be? Population rises to nearly 11,000 million by 2300, and then levels out. Why does it level out? – because *food* has become the limiting factor. Forrester[3] formalizes this as a sort of Parkinsonian principle: 'If all other influences on growth are removed, the population will rise by as much as necessary to generate the degree of food shortage that is needed to suppress growth.'

You can go on playing with the model and juggling with your assumptions for as long as you like: it will keep on coming out with the same kinds of conclusions. And all of them centre on one simple fact: that regardless of what we choose to do or to leave undone, within the next century the whole tenor of the human way of life is going to be transformed; the 'growth' mode will give way to an 'equilibrium' one. And this is a transformation that we have never previously had to contemplate.

Cities, as we have noted, are systems; and in some respects they represent a miniature of the world system. At their founding land is cheap and abundant, and they grow rapidly. As horizontal space becomes filled up they begin to utilize vertical space. Population density in the city centre rises, necessitating the development of enormous and complex systems of public transport. The central area becomes a less pleasant place to inhabit; rich people move out to the ever-spreading suburbs. Finally, when the city grows chronically large, it begins to equilibrate; the population stops growing, as it has in New York, in Chicago, in Philadelphia.

But in one important respect a city is not a real parallel of the world system. It achieves its equilibrium not by ceasing to produce people, but by producing them and exporting them. In spite of this relatively easy option no one could say that the achievement of equilibrium by cities has not been a shatteringly painful process, psychologically, socially, and economically. It has involved inflation, unemployment, slums, ghettoes, pollution, noise, drug addiction, crime, and a host of other things. What, then, are we to expect of the world transformation, where the 'easy way out' – export of surplus people to new land – is not an available option?

The world model gives us a few ideas about what to expect. It tells us that equilibrium is coming, regardless of what decisions we make now, regardless of what actions or policies we institute. But it also tells us that there is a measure of choice regarding the way in which equilibrium comes about. It tells us that we can either usher in equilibrium ourselves, by designing and carrying out certain programmes; or we can simply wait passively for it to arrive, by collapse of our resource base, by runaway pollution, by starvation, or whatever. But what shall we have to do to contrive and control the transformation; if in fact that is the choice we make?

The model has already told us a few things which we *cannot* do and expect them to result in equilibrium. What is the single most striking feature of the 'world system' today? – it is the imbalance between birth rate and death rate, the astronomical number of births. And remember what social systems do: they tend to draw attention to inherently insensitive parts of themselves. The birth rate is such a factor: it is an ineffective point at which to apply leverage to the system. We may assume that if a birth control programme is ever going to be effective it will be effective in conditions of near-starvation, high pollution levels, extreme overcrowding, and low quality of life. These are the pressures which might generate enough momentum to get a birth control programme launched. But a birth control programme will reduce these pressures, and increase the influences which tend to raise the birth rate: more food, more space, less pollution. A birth control programme will be inherently self-defeating unless we introduce new pressures to replace the ones we have alleviated.

What if we follow Commoner and Coale and forget about birth control, concentrating instead on cutting down on our consumption of natural resources? What will happen, as we have seen, is that the population crash will be postponed for a few years, but when it does come it will be far more severe, reducing population to something less than a thousand million, or what it was in about 1800. A resource slowdown alone would in fact be a thoroughly irresponsible and malicious policy to follow; its major effect would be to achieve a many-fold worsening of our problems.

So what shall we have to do, then? How are we going to stop the curves on Forrester's graphs from rocketing upwards or plummeting downwards; how are we going to cause them to level out, to equilibrate? Here's how Forrester did it in the *World Dynamics* model. Starting in 1970, we decide to hold the material standard of living at today's level. We reduce our rate of usage of natural resources by 75 per cent. We reduce pollution generation by 50 per cent. We reduce capital-investment generation by 40 per cent. We reduce the birthrate by 40 per cent. And we *reduce* food production by 20 per cent (remember that stuff about replacing old pressures by new ones? Present pressures result in growth; we have to replace them by equally strong ones which will lead to equi-librium).

L.G.

F

And what is the result of all this? It brings about a world in which many of our old gods are dead and gone forever: population growth, rising standards of living, resource development. It means a reduction in the investment rate and a reduction in agricultural productivity; both of which, as Forrester drily notes, are counter-intuitive. Such policies, he further acknowledges,[3] 'are not likely to be accepted without . . . years of argument – perhaps more years than are available'.

Damn right, too! Just who is going to accept policies like those? – nobody that I know of, not even the Club of Rome. Here is the version of the equilibrium model that they have endorsed, derived from the washed-and-polished second version of the world model.[5]

Zero population growth (the birth rate equals the death rate) is introduced in 1975. Industrial capital is stabilized in 1990. Resource consumption is reduced by 75 per cent in 1975. Also in 1975, the material standard of living is stabilized, pollution generation is reduced to 25 per cent of the 1970 value, massive investment is made in food production and simultaneously in maintaining soil fertility, and the average lifetime of industrial capital is greatly increased, by phasing out planned obsolescence and phasing in durability. After all this has happened we find ourselves in a world where there is more than twice as much food available per person, where average world income has tripled, where industrial output and services per head are well above today's levels. (One is tempted to inquire, in this situation, what it is that keeps the birth rate down.)

Never mind about that for the moment: let's stand back and try to get an overall view of what has come out of this grand exercise in computer wizardry. The final impression left is one of sadness: sadness not only for ourselves but primarily for the Club of Rome and the computer jockeys. There they were: they set out with the highest of ideals, the best of intentions. They called on the wisest brains, the hottest technology, that the world could offer. They invested their time, their energy, their money; they sought no profits or powers for themselves. And what is the outcome? All they have succeeded in doing is showing, clearly and explicitly, that the solution to the Predicament of Man is infinitely, inconceivably more difficult than we thought before they set to work. The kinds of solutions they offer are really no more than conceptual, intellectual, academic possibilities. Your finger is hurting so you cut off your arm: that is the kind of solution they represent.

But perhaps you doubt the validity of these computer models; perhaps you can't accept some of the assumptions they make. You could easily talk me into agreeing with you, and we would be in profuse company: taking pot-shots at Jay Forrester and the Club of Rome is rapidly becoming a favourite indoor sport. Thomas Boyle,[6] for instance, announced triumphantly in September 1973 that he had found a typographic error in one of the *Limits to Growth* programmes. He eliminated the error, and on re-running the programme found that a 'pollution crisis' outcome did not result from the 'technological fix' simulation. There is hope for the technological solution after all, concluded Boyle; technological fixes could lead to 'a satisfactory transition to a stabilized comfortable world'.

It is thoroughly pleasing, of course, to find that even computer whiz-kids can make typographic errors. But in January 1974 Meadows and Meadows[4] (two of the authors of *The Limits to Growth*), while admitting the mistake, pointed out that it had 'had only a small quantitative effect on the published results. The error was not responsible for the pollution crisis mode; its removal does not stabilize the model system and the conclusions are unaffected by the numerical change. *Touché.*

The comments of some other critics [7] [8] [9] lead one to wonder whether their disapproval of the model stems from the fact that it clashes with their preconceptions; or whether it really is, as a critic in *Science*[10] put it, 'blatant and insensitive advocacy for unsubstantiated model building on a very large scale'; with a 'behavioural-scientific content [of] virtually zero'. Of course there are valid criticisms to be made; it is undeniable, for instance, that the model is too 'coarse'; it treats a variable and heterogeneous world as though it were uniform. Nevertheless – however much one may quibble about particular points – through all the maze of flows and levels, of curves and formulae, of multipliers and normals, two general things stand out. One is that the computer-generated model, regardless of whether it's better or worse, is at least *different* from our orthodox mental models. It came into being in a different way; it used new techniques and recently-acquired skills. For all that its conclusions do not differ radically from those that many people have arrived at by less esoteric paths. Someone hands you a piece of an unknown substance and asks you to work out what it is. You analyse it chemically and conclude that it's a piece of wood. Someone else cuts sections of it and studies them under a microscope – a new approach, a different technique – and announces that it's a piece of bone. That would really shake your faith in your wood hypothesis; but that isn't what's happened in this case. The microscopist, like the chemist, has no doubt whatever that the thing is wood. The systems analyst, like the ecologist, is unshakeably of the opinion that the world as we know it is rapidly coming to an end.

A second, and more immediate, achievement of the system dynamics merchant is summed up by the title of Forrester's

1970 paper in *Technology Review*: 'The Counterintuitive Behaviour of Social Systems'.[1] This, as we have seen, is one of the most striking conclusions of the system dynamics approach. It means that to influence the behaviour of our social systems we shall have to adopt counterintuitive policies; policies which seem wrong, policies which go against the grain, policies which are immoral, illiberal, anti-humanitarian; policies which are the precise opposite of *doing the logical thing*. If we were pinning our faith on obvious solutions – better technology, birth control, food from the sea – we can forget about it. Even if you believe that they are attainable (which, as we have seen, is improbable), they are *non*-solutions: they will leave the problems untouched, or, more commonly, make them worse.

How ready are we to accept counterintuitive philosophies? Here's a test case. In *New Scientist* for 23 March 1972 Alec Nisbett[11] wrote an article in which he demolished the 'myth' of Lake Erie: that it is a dead lake, killed by pollution. On the contrary, he noted, it is so alive that it supports a fishing industry which measures its catch in thousands of tons annually. He enjoyed several excellent meals of Lake Erie fish; even a biologist working on mercury pollution in a neighbouring lake unhesitatingly ate fish from Lake Erie.

What does Nisbett conclude from this? That the pollution scare has been exaggerated, of course; that the ecologists have been crying wolf. And perhaps he's right. But that isn't really the question at issue. The question is: is the fact that Lake Erie is still alive a good thing for the future of mankind? He doesn't answer that one: he tacitly (intuitively) assumes that the answer is *Yes*.

But what if we look at the situation counterintuitively? We could reason something like this: Lake Erie is still alive – in spite of all the mistreatment it's been subjected to, in spite of all the poisons that have been dumped into it – it remains alive. Therefore we can conclude that gross abuse of lakes is quite OK, and we shall carry on with it. We can safely industrialize more, dump more, foul our nest more, and get away with it. We can go on as we have been for years and years yet; no problem at all.

But if Lake Erie really had died, what then? Mightn't it have worried us just a little? Mightn't we have thought: now that we've gone and demolished a whole bloody lake hadn't we better think again about what we're doing? Mightn't it have been a demonstration *par excellence* that we were in all kinds of trouble? Mightn't it have been the one thing that could force us to take stock of the situation; to reflect not on the future of Lake Erie but on the future of mankind?

But Nisbett, not surprisingly and by no means alone, is unable to contemplate Lake Erie in a counterintuitive frame of mind. He retains boundless faith in the good old technological fix, in an orthodox solution to an orthodox problem. He concludes his article by saying that the lesson to be learned from Lake Erie is that it

> 'created a situation where scientists may be shown by events to have cried "wolf". Dr Paul Ehrlich tries to get out of this . . . by saying that if he's wrong it doesn't matter – but if he's right, the world may be saved. But that will not wash. We have to save the world anyway – and I follow Dr Commoner in believing that we will recognize the problems that face us and will set about solving them. But, at the same time, we cannot evade the need to consider other problems – and the high cost of dealing with them: we must solve our environmental problems with a proper regard for other demands on the public purse. Which means that once the initial impetus has been given, what the public needs from the scientists is guidance . . . in what exactly needs to be done and how best to do it.'

From all of which I am sure you will derive a great deal of comfort.

Let's look at another pollution problem on a smaller scale. It is a safe bet that your city has a litter problem: what is it doing about it? No doubt it's spending more on rubbish collection services, on street cleaning and the like. That is the logical thing to do; and it is, of course, self-defeating. The city authorities are asking, and answering, the wrong question. The problem is not, how are we going to dispose of all this rubbish? It is, how can we stop all this rubbish being produced? Providing more rubbish-disposal services simply relaxes any pressure there might be to hold down the rubbish-generation rate: it ensures that *more* rubbish will be generated. Needless to say very few cities have come to this counterintuitive conclusion.

What do we do if we hear that thousands of people are starving to death in some far away Third World country? The logical and humane thing is to send them food, so that's what we do. Hence it isn't surprising to find that what this basically achieves is an aggravation of the food shortage. The arrival of large quantities of rice or wheat or whatever at a port attracts people to the port; they leave the countryside and migrate to the already crowded city. So there is a decrease in primary productivity and an increase in the dependent urban portion of the population; the capacity of the country to produce food for itself is diminished. Also, of course, it gives the impression that a country's inability to feed itself doesn't matter, because there is a cornucopia somewhere which can happily keep despatching ships filled with grain. And finally, it removes a pressure which would in the longer term help to achieve population stability; it negates the approximate parity between a country's population and its food-producing capability.

Let's go on to a less disturbing example. In Australia for

some time there has been an active union campaign going on for the 40-hour working week to be replaced by a 35-hour week. It is particularly vigorous in situations where there has been substantial automation, such as on the docks and in power generation. The reason is logical enough: the introduction of automation has resulted in an excess of man-hours so we'll reduce the surplus by decreasing the number of hours. Which is one way, and the obvious way, of doing it. But the only way to achieve a long-term reduction would be to concentrate on the *men*, not the *hours*; to stabilize the work-force by limiting the number of men. We are not, needless to say, contemplating this possibility; neither the unions nor the governments who are opposing them.

We could go on multiplying examples for some time, but there is little point. We have seen enough to be able to appreciate the brass tacks of the system analyst's argument. He is telling us that, regardless of whether it is theoretically possible to influence the behaviour of the world and its component social systems, we are unable to influence it for the better by applying obvious, commonsense, it-goes-without-saying policies, by doing the logical thing. What we must do is be cruel to be kind, fly in the face of logic, go against our better judgement, deny the validity of our own powers of reasoning. We must be inhumane, undemocratic, unfair. We must keep food from starving people; we must tread on aspirations and ambitions. We cannot control the birth rate, for instance, by making it easy *not* to have children; it can be done only by making it hard, or unpleasant, or traumatic, to have them.

So we have come back to Garrett Hardin's[12] point again: there is a class of problems which have no technical solution. The arms race is a member of this class; so is racism; so are crime and unemployment; and so is the Predicament of Man. We are not going to save the world by any technical fixes, no matter how far-reaching or costly we are prepared to make them. We are not going to feed the world merely by growing more food, or control populations simply by presenting them with contraceptives. What is about to occur is a drastic, unprecedented, unimaginable revolution in the world of man: the transition from growth to equilibrium. If we are to have any say in its manner of coming about then there must be a prior revolution in ourselves. We shall have to alter the definition of *moral* so that it comes to include nearly everything we now label *immoral*. Our new definition of *humane* will have most of the attributes of our old *inhumane*. Likewise *selfless* will change places with *selfish*, *liberal* with *repressive*, *democratic* with *totalitarian*. We shall have to turn ourselves and our institutions inside-out, upside-down, back-to-front. We shall have to make the French Revolution look like a damp squib; the Russian Revolution like a children's tea party.

'Like everybody else,' wrote Charles Fort[13] regarding another matter, 'I have my own notions upon what constitutes reasonableness . . .' That is as good an epitaph as any for the contribution of system dynamics to the salvation of mankind. Is it reasonable to ask people to kindly treat themselves as robots, to switch off their ambitions and emotions, to behave in ways which are selected on the basis of whether they make a graph go up or down? Is it reasonable to say, Yes, you *can* save those people from death, but you *mustn't*. To say, Certainly you *can* halve the pollution output of that factory, but you're forbidden to, unless you simultaneously . . .? Is it a real argument to say: You must allow that child to starve to death in front of your eyes – don't worry about it – in forty years' time it will *save* lives? You must not irrigate that land to produce desperately-needed crops. You must deny the reasonable use of electrical energy to millions of people. You must ruthlessly crush any strivings by anybody to achieve a better life-style for themselves.

You must apply a cure which is as bad as the disease; that is what it amounts to. Worse, actually, for the reason that Garrett Hardin[14] gave in his *Science* editorial quoted in Chapter 6. If, to take just one example, we deliberately withhold food from starving people we shall find it hard to escape the horror, the sin, the guilt . . . *we* killed those people. But if we simply let things ride along, take their course, we shall neatly manage to avoid this uncomfortable self-accusation. It will be a drought that kills them, or a flood, or an epidemic, or *something*. But not some*one*, not us.

And that, when you think about it, is a perfectly valid and reasonable justification for the policy we have resolutely decided to follow: to do nothing at all . . .

NOTES

1 FORRESTER, JAY W. 'Counterintuitive Behaviour of Social Systems', *Technology Review*, Vol. 73 (1971) 1-16

2 FORRESTER, JAY W. *Urban Dynamics* (The M.I.T. Press 1969)

3 FORRESTER, JAY W. *World Dynamics* (Wright-Allen Press 1971)

4 MEADOWS, D. H., and MEADOWS, D. L. 'Typographical Errors and Technological Solutions', *Nature*, Vol. 247 (1974) 97-98

5 MEADOWS, D. H., MEADOWS, D. L., RANDERS, J., *and* BEHRENS, W. W. *The Limits to Growth* (London, Earth Island 1972)

6 BOYLE, THOMAS J. 'Hope for the Technological Solution', *Nature*, Vol. 245 (1973) 127-28

7 BOYD, ROBERT. 'World Dynamics: A Note', *Science*, Vol. 177 (1972) 516-19

8 ANON. 'More Coals of Fire for Club of Rome', *Nature*, Vol. 239 (1972) 248-49

9 STREATFIELD, GUY. 'No Limit to the Growth Debate', *New Scientist*, Vol. 57 (1973) 531-33

10 SHUBIK, M. 'Modeling on a Grand Scale', *Science*, Vol. 174 (1971) 1014-15

11 NISBETT, ALEC. 'The Myth of Lake Erie', *New Scientist*, Vol. 53 (1972) 650-53

12 HARDIN, GARRETT. 'The Tragedy of the Commons', *Science*, Vol. 162 (1968) 1243-48

13 FORT, CHARLES. *New Lands* (New York, Holt, Rinehart and Winston 1941)

14 HARDIN, GARRETT. 'Nobody Ever Dies of Overpopulation', *Science*, Vol. 171 (1971) Editorial

9 Never Give Up, All Will Be Well, We're The Boss

> 'I believe nothing of my own that I have ever written.'
> Charles Fort: *Lo!*

At this stage of the proceedings you may well have decided that I have worked myself into a corner from which I cannot escape. On the one hand I've said that the human race will not acknowledge the reality of what is about to happen to it, and on the other that I *do* acknowledge it. *Ergo*, I cannot be a member of the human race. How am I going to extricate myself from that one?

I'm not going to try. Rather, I am going to allow that, like every other person on earth, I really consist of two people: the intellectual me and the emotional me. The intellectual me is convinced of the truth of what I have written, but the emotional me won't have it. The emotional me simply refuses to contemplate any part of it, much less believe it. This doesn't surprise me, or alarm me, or worry me. Unlike Arthur Koestler,[1] I do not deduce that 'man's native equipment . . . may contain some serious faults in the circuitry of his most precious and delicate instrument – the central nervous system'. On the contrary, I think it very clever of my brain to have such an efficient method of handling and classifying information. God knows what sort of a mental wreck I'd be if my wily little central nervous system were *not* able to do this for me.

I remember, as a schoolboy in South Africa, coming up

against the intellectual problem of racism. I went to some school club meeting or other – perhaps it was a debate – where the subject of racial equality reared its head. Afterwards I walked back to my dormitory with the school's head prefect. He was fully seventeen, and I was only fifteen: what a gulf of intellectual maturity between us! I remember nervously venturing something like: 'I think racial discrimination is bloody stupid, don't you . . . I mean, I think the Africans are as good as us . . .'

'Of course,' he replied, 'but have you ever thought of it this way? Suppose you arrive at a hotel late at night, and you want a bed. The manager tells you, "I'm sorry – I have only one bed empty, and it was slept in by an African last night. The laundry hasn't arrived today so the same linen is still on the bed, but you can sleep in it if you want to." The African, you may assume, was a clean, decent clergyman, probably better educated than either of us.

'Would you sleep in the bed?'

In reply I think I said something like, 'Oh, I . . . er . . . well, I . . . um . . .' Years later I thought of what would have been a bold and forthright reply; and one that had the advantage of neatly avoiding the issue: 'No, I wouldn't; but then I wouldn't if it had been a white person who'd used the bed either.' Later still I realized that his argument was just a simple trick: converting an intellectual issue into an emotional one. The old 'Would you like your daughter to marry one?' gambit, nothing more.

The point is that it is the emotional messages which really have an impact on us. Suppose you hear on the radio one day that eight South Vietnamese children have 'accidentally' been killed in a napalm attack; I doubt that you do more than pause in your stride for a moment. But if you see the same item on a television newsreel, with film of the scalded, dying children running screaming out of the flames, you are probably upset enough not to feel like finishing your dinner. And finally: imagine if you had been there, in the midst of the smoke and the screams and the scorching flesh. What would you have been feeling then? In each case the emotional impact is progressively greater, and the effect on you therefore increasingly disturbing.

This is a trick which is well known to advertisers, of course. Don't say *soft*, say *kitten-soft* (warm, cuddly); don't say *greasy*, say *with smooth, aromatic oils* (sensuous, sexy); and so it goes on. Messages with emotional appeal are the ones that get across. By the same token, communications which are lacking in this kind of appeal tend to be ignored. It isn't a question of not believing them; it's simply that they do not have the same effect on your central nervous system.

In part all this is no doubt related to our double system of communication. We are the only creatures possessing a language: a learned system of innately meaningless symbols which we use to represent things. Other animals can only communicate actualities: I am a male, I hold this territory; or emotional states: I am ready to mate, I am about to attack. We might call this 'emotional' communication, as opposed to 'intellectual' communication (language), and although we have patented the latter system we have by no means abandoned the former. Most of our really vital messages – those concerned with such things as love, anger, fear and hatred – still have a substantial unlearned, emotional component in them. We supplement our fancy, acquired language with that good old animal system of non-symbolic communication: touching hands, clenching fists, screaming, grinding teeth, or whatever. If someone says to you, quietly and calmly, 'I hate you', you probably feel a little uncomfortable about it. But if he shrieks 'I hate you' in a howl of frenzied rage, and at the same time goes red in the face, pounds his fists on the table, and froths at the mouth, you not only feel uncomfortable – you get the hell out of there, fast.

Herein resides my ability to write un-human things and still claim to be a member of the human race. I contemplate what I have written *intellectually*; there are but few topics mentioned here which have an immediate *emotional* impact on me. *My* children aren't starving; *my* country isn't grossly overpopulated; *my* atmosphere isn't toxic enough for me to have to wear an oxygen mask when I walk down the street. Barely any of this has yet touched me emotionally and I cannot therefore speak for people whom it *has*. The intellectual 'I' is proud of the convincing case he thinks he has made; the emotional 'I' does not believe a word of his own that he has written.

But we do more than just ignore nasty and threatening messages: we are positively optimistic about them. Being eternal optimists has been a very significant factor in our survival. If one had to summarize the bulk of our evolutionary history in a single word that word would have to be *struggle*. We asked for it, after all; we were basically a frugivorous forest-dweller who abandoned his friendly and familiar habitat for the hostile world of the savannah and the hunter. We couldn't have expected a path strewn with rose petals, and we certainly didn't get one. If there was one law of survival in this rat-race it was: never give up. No matter how bad things seem, keep going, keep struggling, keep fighting.

We need only compare two hypothetical groups of palaeolithic men to see how vitally important this would have been. These groups, like all others at the time, tottered along from crisis to crisis, disaster to disaster. Recall some of the things we have deduced about them, such as child mortality of at least one in two and a maximum life span of twenty to thirty years.* These were grim, heartbreaking times, when adults

* It is an astonishing fact that the *average* expectation of life in

died violent deaths and the child mortality rate was horrifying. There must have been innumerable occasions when the situation was clearly so absolutely hopeless that by far the best strategy seemed to be to crawl into your cave and die; and perhaps one of our groups did. And what happened to them? – they sank without trace; they left no descendants. It was the tough ones, the resilient ones, the optimistic ones, who survived and contributed to later generations; the ones who refused to give in no matter how impossible the odds. Optimism is built into us; the pessimists (*real* pessimists) amongst us were weeded out many generations ago. Only optimists survived.

No wonder, then, that we have such a phenomenal ability to ignore the doomsday merchants. That was the way we got here; it's what we have always done. It has never done anyone any good, listening to the defeatists; even if they're right, you see, you can't do yourself any harm by refusing to heed them.

The uphill battle that we have had has left another legacy which is exerting an enormous influence on our way of life today. For we were never, needless to say, content to merely *survive* crises; our technique was to survive them and then *conquer* them. We were up against an environment which kept launching new hostilities at us: droughts, floods, starvation, heat, cold, beasts of prey. But one after another we overcame them and took them in our stride. We had to hunt for food, so we invented weapons. We found that the weather was often unpredictable, so we built dams and canals. We found ourselves beset by diseases, until we thought up antidotes: medicines, surgery, antibiotics. *Struggle*: that was the key. We struggled to survive, and whenever possible to

---

sixteenth century England was of the order of eight and a half years.[2]

dominate, our hostile surroundings. Lionel Tiger[3] lists aggression against the environment as one of his major categories of aggressive activity; and indeed, why not? The environment was out to get us, and small wonder that we got it instead on every possible occasion.

If you have made your name, your reputation, your fortune, as, say, a concert pianist, you would be rather stupid to drop everything and turn to bricklaying for a living. Indeed, you would probably find it an impossible transition. Likewise *Homo sapiens* as a whole: he got where he is by dominating his environment, by making it dance to his tune; must he now do an abrupt about-face? Must he say: I became human because I subjugated my environment, but being human I must cease subjugating it?

The heart of the matter is the drastic change that has taken place in our ability to turn our environment to our own purposes. Our australopithecine, or *Homo erectus*, or palaeolithic or neolithic *Homo sapiens*, could just about keep one jump ahead by fighting his environment tooth and nail. The gardeners of the Tsembaga are an example: their exploitation of the rainforest consists in scratching a few temporary clearings. They lack the means, the machinery, the energy resources, to do more than that. If we, on the other hand, set out to exploit a rainforest, we can do exactly as we please. We can cut it to the ground if we want to, and hardly exert ourselves in the process. We can even, given a little longer, take away the very mountain on which the forest stands, and use it to fill in a valley somewhere else. Because of our history we still fight our environment with every trick we know; the trouble is that we can now beat hell out of it with one hand tied behind our backs, and it has had more than it can take. And added to this is the fact that there are now so many more of us: so many additional straws for the camel's back.

So what is happening now is not really a reflection of any change in our philosophy since those far-off camp fire days. We are doing the same things as we always did, only doing them a lot more effectively. We cannot say, if only we could bring back the good old days; revert to our way of life of 1000 BC, or AD 1000, or 1200, or 1500, or what you will . . . We were living then by the same token as we live now: we are human, we are dominant, we are the boss.

Jane Goodall's[4] remarkable studies of chimpanzees have told us a great deal about the behaviour of these splendid primates, and, by analogy, about that of early hominids. They do so many of the things that we have been speculating that our ancestors must have done . . . they make and use tools to help collect food and water; they hunt down, kill and eat smaller creatures; they have a highly-organized system of social relationships and communication. Yet one of the most poignant sections of Goodall's delightful *In the Shadow of Man* is also the section which reveals one of the major differences between the pongid apes and ourselves, the hominids. What do they do when their environment suddenly turns nasty and lashes out at them, maiming and killing? They fall, helpless, before it. During Dr Goodall's study a polio epidemic broke out among her chimps, and she was subjected to the harrowing experience of watching her familiar and beloved animals being turned into crippled, stinking, bleeding monstrosities, living in torment and dying in agony. And the chimps, makers of drinking sponges and of termite catchers, constructors of extraordinarily neat and cosy sleeping nests, were utterly powerless to do anything about it.

Dr Goodall, of course, was not. She set about the epidemic with vaccine-laced bananas, and saved the lives of who knows how many chimps. Polio is an environmental hazard, like so many others, which we can handle; chimpanzees are creatures, like all others on earth except ourselves, which lack all but the most trivial of cultural guns which can be brought to bear on a besieging environment.

It is important to note that it is just this difference which sets us apart from all other organisms. Each of them, each of us, are doing our level best to adapt to our environment as thoroughly as we can. We are not doing anything different from them: we are doing the same things, only vastly more effectively. Every creature tries to turn its environment to its own ends as much as possible, but most of them lack the wherewithal to achieve anything very substantial. Beavers build their dams, yes, and termites their huge and complex mounds; the cactus finch plucks a thorn with which to probe for insects and the sea otter uses a stone to smash open shellfish. Puny efforts, at best. But it is a safe assumption that, given our advantages, they would be just as dictatorial towards their environment as we are towards ours (just as the Tsembaga gardener achieves conservative usage of his forests; not because he wants to but because he has no option. Given the means he would doubtless have wrecked them as fast as we wrecked ours). Any other creature could attempt to do what we do, but no other has the combination of characteristics which has been our path to glory: an upright stance, a superb brain, skilful hands, and all the rest of it. It is interesting to speculate what that lord of the oceans, the dolphin, might have achieved in the marine world if only he had been endowed with prehensile appendages.

Every organism tries to dominate its environment; we, uniquely, have succeeded. The web of life, the balance of nature, the ecological equilibrium: all are merely summations of the strivings of each individual organism. As we have seen, the whole is no more than the sum of its parts. Other organisms do not achieve stability because they 'want' to; it is simply that no alternative is open to them. We found ourselves with an alternative, and, just as they would have done,

we seized it gratefully and made the most of it. And a highl:
successful most it has been.

Doggedness, optimism, domination: three of the charac
teristics which have made us what we are. There are man:
others, too, but with these three alone we can build up :
complete enough picture of the inevitability of what is t(
befall us.

Doggedness: the *never give up* philosophy. This has had :
thousand and one effects on our behaviour, and we have com(
across a good many of them. We have the ability to cling t(
the most lost of causes, the most unlikely of hypotheses, com(
hell or high water. How long did the search for the Philo-
sopher's Stone last? How many millennia of deforestation,
dust storms and soil erosion has it taken for us to realize that
our agricultural methodology has had serious flaws in it from
the start? For how much longer are we going to perpetuate
the myths of the selflessness of man, the inalienable rights of
man, the immunity of man from negative feedback processes? When are we going to realize that our scarch for
orthodox, comfortable, technical fixes to our crises is a pure
and simple waste of time?

The answer to these questions and many like them is, of
course, never. We do not give up, remember; we do not
admit defeat. Like the spider we try and try again. But when
the spider is finished all she has achieved is a gossamer web;
when we are through we have disfigured a planet. But, again
like the spider, we have perfectly good reasons for our cussedness. Spiders which persevere for long enough succeed in the
end; spiders which give up leave no mark on the world, not
even any baby spiders. We, too, have always succeeded in the
end; and there is no reason in our history to persuade us that
this state of affairs is not going to continue.

There is no question, of course, of our giving up altogether,
of crawling into our caves and waiting for death. But there is

a very persuasive case for giving up some of our strategies, and replacing them by more sensible ones. We should be trying to phase the motor car down to the smallest, most insignificant role we can find for it. Instead we are doing our level best to keep it on its present pedestal of indispensability. We should be cherishing whales as a pathway, the only pathway, which offers us any reasonable hope of extracting the food energy contained in plankton; in reality we are engaged in a cut-throat race to exterminate them. We should be setting our sights on the end of the next century; instead our planning barely extends to the end of this one.

Optimism – the *all will be well* philosophy – is the reason that most of us believe that everything, somehow, despite the myriad indications to the contrary, is going to turn out all right in the end. All we have to do is keep pursuing our present policies; after all, we've done pretty well out of them up to now, haven't we? Jay Forrester[5] believes that the standard of living in Western countries may now be on a crest: the highest it ever has been, the highest it's ever going to be. From now on, he thinks, it will start declining rapidly, because of crowding, because of pollution, because of resource shortages. But the fact remains that our immediate past policies are what brought us to this crest: why should we abandon them now? Is it any wonder that inside, deep down, in our hearts and souls, we do not seriously *want* to extricate ourselves from the mire; that we are not even half-heartedly trying? Saving the giant panda, yes; planting the odd forest, fine; but setting the world on an equilibrium course . . .? That's another thing altogether.

It is also optimism which leads the Forresters, the Ehrlichs, the Commoners, to make the suggestions for saving the world that they do: optimism that someone will take some notice of them. Their built-in optimism allows them seriously to entertain the possibility that the world is going to launch itself enthusiastically into a Club of Rome type revolution. I permits them to write books the first two thirds of which tel us why we've had it; the last third why we haven't. In this a least Paul Ehrlich and Colin Clark do not differ; both have recipes for the salvation of mankind.

We do, after all, have compelling reasons for being optimistic: we have defied a number of supposedly omnipoten principles and got away with it. What, for instance, is the central thread of evolutionary theory, the one that everybody can quote? It is *survival of the fittest*. In other words, those lineages with the greatest fitness survive; those with lesser fitness do not. And what is fitness? — it is the ability to have offspring, which is a reflection of how good one's adaptation to the environment is. And adaptation to the environment is in turn compounded of a number of factors: ability to survive unfavourable conditions, ability to find food and attract a mate, and so on. Thus as a general rule those who are physically fittest also have the greatest evolutionary fitness; except, it goes without saying, in man. We have succeeded in almost entirely divorcing physical and evolutionary fitness; the two need no longer be related. A diabetic can have children, a deaf-mute, a cripple, a haemophiliac; we have given the power to have progeny to all of them. And that is a very big achievement indeed, far greater than sending men to the moon; if we can do that what can't we do?

And then domination: the philosophy of *we're the boss*. The philosophy that anything which represents additional mastery over the environment is *good*, to the point where domination turns into destruction. This is truly our crowning glory: it was what started us off on the human road; it is what is maintaining us as kings of the castle today. It is not surprising that we now equate *domination* with *progress*, even when the outcome cannot be interpreted as progress in any meaningful sense of the word. I remember seeing a fascinatng television documentary about a Western medical team which set up shop in an African village, and instituted a programme of child nutrition and health care. The results were spectacular: child mortality fell by half. The environment was hostile – it made children sick, it killed them – and the medicos set out to, and did, dominate the causes of mortality. Progress, of course; but my first thought on watching the documentary was: What effect is this increased survival rate *now* going to have on the *adult* mortality rate in ten or fifteen years' time, and on the mortality of *their* children?

Another example on a more trivial but familiar scale: perhaps you drive to work along a freeway. Now a freeway, in numerous ways that I can think of, is a backward step from the rutted cart-track that it replaced. The freeway is less attractive, more destructive of land, noisier, less healthy, more consuming of energy, more likely to kill you, and (in peak hours, at least) slower. We create a shambles: a modern city, with its monumental traffic problems; we then construct freeways, which initially achieve a marginal un-shambling of the situation, and later make it worse; and to crown our achievement we label the whole comedy 'progress'. A freeway does not represent progress in any obvious sense of the word, but it *does* represent additional domination, and that is why it is good. The same point was pithily made by the president of an American consumer association in bemoaning the unreliability of modern electrical appliances: 'When a $300 fully-automatic washing machine with whistles and bells on it won't run properly, it's not as effective as the medieval practice of beating clothes on rocks'.[6]

It is time to summarize our arguments. Where we differ from the rest of the biotic world is that we live by a growth code, they by an equilibrium one. And *why* we differ is not that we set out to do different things; we had the same aims.

But whereas they, by and large, failed, we have gloriously splendidly, triumphantly succeeded. Had any of them possessed our bag full of tricks they, too, might have ruled the earth; in fact the ones among them which have been the most successful are those which have parasitized *our* success: the rat, the cockroach, the housefly. But every other organism in its own way is optimistic, is persistent, and strives to dominate its environment; and what results is mere survival if it is lucky. This point was again brought home to me by that wise and wonderful animal, the chimpanzee. The Melbourne Zoo is gradually becoming a place of fine, open, grassy enclosures, but there are still a few of the older steel-and-concrete horrors housing its inmates. Up until recently one of them was the chimpanzee cage: a small, dark, cold, featureless dungeon. And Melbourne's winter does not help much, being notoriously cold and wet, with biting winds. How much further can you get from the tropical African forest than this dank and cheerless prison? And yet Molly, an old female chimp, still managed to bear an infant one recent midwinter's day. Again, how much more optimistic, more persevering, more defiant, can you be than to try to perpetuate your lineage in such conditions? But Molly, of course, is a mere ape, and the next day her baby was dead.

Persistence, optimism, domination: let's reduce these three terms to one now; we can label it *domination*, since this is the major factor which engenders optimism and persistence in us. It is also the single characteristic which marks the greatest gulf between ourselves and other living organisms. They, too, are optimistic; they are persistent; and they struggle with their environment, but they do not *dominate* it. Their environment is the piper to whose tune they dance; we, in the most spectacular reversal of roles ever achieved, have made the environment dance to ours.

It is instructive to note, in this regard, the criteria which

we use to identify domination by other members of the
animal kingdom. We call the lion 'the king of the beasts'.
Why? Because, presumably, we have an image of it rampag-
ing around devouring whomsoever it pleases without being
answerable to any higher authority. Or consider the dinosaurs: the 'terrible lizards', the 'ruling reptiles', the 'giants
of the earth'. Why do we always think of them as having
'ruled the world'? Again, one can only assume it is because
the most memorable among them were huge, and powerful,
and fearsome; probably dealing as they pleased with any of
their contemporaries who dared to get in their way.

And yet the other phrase which springs irresistibly to mind
in association with dinosaurs is 'magnificent failures'. *Failures*, we must suppose, since having ruled the earth for a
while they were utterly obliterated, and vanished abruptly
from the scene. But 'for a while' represents a span of some
100 million years; just one kind of dinosaur, *Iguanodon*, was
around for something of the order of 55 million years. What
can we claim for man? A quarter of a million years. For the
genus *Homo*: Three million. Well what about *Australopithecus* + *Homo*? Still only five or six million, I'm afraid.
Perhaps we should withhold our judgement of the success or
failure of *Iguanodon* (relative to ourselves) until the year
50,001,975 or thereabouts.

The simple fact is that *Iguanodon* pressed on for the very
reason that it did *not* rule the earth; on the contrary, it
allowed the earth to rule it. It did not dominate, but it *did*
survive, for a span of time whose vastness we cannot begin to
comprehend. And the obvious moral of the story is: if you
want to survive, don't dominate, don't rule the world.

This is precisely what everyone is telling us, of course. We
must reduce by 75 per cent the natural resource usage rate,
says the Club of Rome. We must reduce food production by
20 per cent, says Forrester. We must reduce our material

wants, our individual wealth, our freedom to exploit, say Ehrlich and Harriman; just as we must give up altogether the concepts of growth, of competition, of progress. We must cease to send aid to grossly overpopulated countries, say the Paddock brothers;[7] we must relinquish the freedom to breed, says Garrett Hardin.

You see what it is that we are being asked to give up: it is *domination*. And in the same breath we are being told that we must abandon our optimism; we must confess that all *won't* be well. And we must also divest ourselves of our sacred notion of never give up; and set up in its place a new statute: we *must* give up our present way of life.

Here's a little sample of what we must strain every nerve and muscle to achieve. We want a society in which growth of GNP has slowed down. We want industries to cut down on production; we want mining companies to ease off on exploration. We want fewer cars to be made and sold, and a cutback in consumption of every other kind. Inevitably at first this will bring unemployment, which we shall welcome as a sign that we are moving in the right direction. We want building, expanding, growing, enlarging, to begin to disappear; we must have a reduction in all kinds of output and material usage.

Now what does all that add up to? It adds up to precisely the situation that Australia found itself in a couple of years ago; it adds up to what Australia promptly labelled a 'recession' (or, in some quarters, a depression). It adds up to exactly the sort of direction that the ZPG'ers, the Save-the-Earthers, the ecologists and the conservationists have been telling us we should be moving in. It adds up to the belief that there is hope after all! They said it couldn't be done, and we are doing it! The Battle is Won—the Predicament is Over!

Not one person in Australia, to my knowledge, said any of

that: not the ZPG merchants, nor the conservationists, nor the Friends of the Earth, nor anyone. And if some hardy soul had ventured a murmur along those lines it would have been drowned in the tumult and the shouting of gloom! gloom! gloom! – How can we stimulate the enonomy? How can we create more jobs? How can we attract investment, increase production, get things moving again? How, in fact, can we *get off equilibrium* (or rather, stagnation) *and back on to growth once more?*

It just cannot be, you see. We are asking the leopard to change his spots, the concert pianist to become a bricklayer. We are being told that everything that has been favoured during our long evolutionary struggle is suddenly wrong, evil, despicable. We are the young Beethoven being told never to compose music, the young Wren never to design a building, the young Shakespeare never to put pen to paper.

This must be our new creed: we do not believe that we are essentially different from any other creature on earth. We should confess that our glorious adventure has ended in failure. We should renounce any suggestion that we can or ought to dominate our environment. We should be less optimistic and persistent and, at the same time, less egocentric and arrogant. We should in fact speak out and say that we are prepared even to abandon some of the most striking aspects of our humanity: we should declare that we shall no longer be human in the full sense of the word as we use it now.

Which, as a general conclusion, is of course a classic case of the evolutionary biologist's typical unhelpfulness, his impracticality, his irresponsibility. And why will it be so judged? – because it gives us nowhere to seek for solutions except in ourselves, in our nature, in our very souls and spirits. It leaves us alone, comfortless, on the brink of the chasm, with only ourselves to contemplate, with no one to appeal to for salvation. There are no more 'experts' to come and rescue us:

these are matters in which *there are no experts*. All our skills, all our marvellous wizardry, are in increasing growth, increasing exploitation, increasing populations . . . in increasing domination. We are raw recruits at the game of decreasing it. We are on our own, without experts, without a technological armoury; and the stakes are higher than they have ever been.

NOTES

1 KOESTLER, ARTHUR. *The Ghost in the Machine* (London, Hutchinson 1967)
2 BRIERLEY, JOHN. *A Natural History of Man* (London, Heinemann 1970)
3 TIGER, LIONEL. *Men in Groups* (London, Thomas Nelson 1969)
4 GOODALL, JANE VAN LAWICK. *In the Shadow of Man* (London, Collins 1971)
5 FORRESTER, JAY W. *World Dynamics* (Chichester, Wright-Allen Press 1971)
6 PACKARD, VANCE. *The Waste Makers* (London, Longmans, Green 1961)
7 PADDOCK, WILLIAM, and PADDOCK, PAUL. *Famine – 1975!* (London, Weidenfeld & Nicolson 1967)

Fontana Social Science

Books available include:

African Genesis Robert Ardrey

The Territorial Imperative Robert Ardrey

The Social Contract Robert Ardrey

Racial Minorities Michael Banton

Ideology in Social Science
Edited by Robin Blackburn

The Sociology of Modern Britain
Edited by Eric Butterworth and David Weir

Social Problems of Modern Britain
Edited by Eric Butterworth and David Weir

Men and Work in Modern Britain
Edited by David Weir

Strikes Richard Hyman

The Dominant Man H. Knipe and G. Maclay

Strike at Pilkingtons Tony Lane and Kenneth Roberts

Figuring Out Society Ronald Meek

Drugs, Science and Society Alan Norton

Dockers David Wilson

Fontana New Naturalist

This series, edited by John Gilmour, Sir Julian Huxley, Margaret Davies and Kenneth Mellanby, was originally published by Collins.

Dartmoor L. A. Harvey & D. St Leger Gordon

The Snowdonia National Park William Condry

The Highlands and Islands F. Fraser Darling and J. Morton Boyd

The Peak District K. C. Edwards

A Natural History of Man in Britain H. J. Fleure and M. Davies

The Trout W. E. Frost and M. E. Brown

Wild Flowers J. Gilmour and M. Walters

The Open Sea: Its Natural History Part One: The World of Plankton Sir Alister Hardy

Insect Natural History A. D. Imms

The Life of the Robin David Lack

Life in Lakes and Rivers T. T. Macan and E. B. Worthington

Climate and the British Scene Gordon Manley

Pesticides and Pollution Kenneth Mellanby

Mountains and Moorlands W. H. Pearsall

The World of the Soil Sir E. John Russell

Britain's Structure and Scenery L. Dudley Stamp

The Sea Shore C. M. Yonge

Fontana Modern Masters

General Editor: Frank Kermode

This series provides authoritative and critical introductions to the most influential and seminal minds of our time. Books already published include:

Beckett   A. Alvarez
Camus   Conor Cruise O'Brien
Chomsky   John Lyons
Einstein   Jeremy Bernstein
Fanon   David Caute
Freud   Richard Wollheim
Gandhi   George Woodcock
Guevara   Andrew Sinclair
Joyce   John Gross
Jung   Anthony Storr
Laing   E. Z. Friedenberg
Lawrence   Frank Kermode
Lenin   Robert Conquest
Lévi-Strauss   Edmund Leach
Lukács   George Lichtheim
Mailer   Richard Poirier
Marcuse   Alasdair MacIntyre
McLuhan   Jonathan Miller
Orwell   Raymond Williams
Popper   Bryan Magee
Reich   Charles Rycroft
Russell   A. J. Ayer
Wittgenstein   David Pears
Yeats   Denis Donoghue

'This series is just what is needed by the so-called "general reader" in search of a guide to intellectual currents that clash so confusingly in a confused world.'

The Times Literary Supplement

Art, Archaeology and Architecture

King Arthur's Avalon   Geoffrey Ashe

The Wonder that was India   A. L. Basham

Italian Painters of the Renaissance
Bernhard Berenson

Citadels of Mystery   L. S. and C. C. de Camp

Goodbye London
Candida Lycett Green and Christopher Booker

Stonehenge Decoded   Gerald S. Hawkins

The Gothic Image   Emile Male

Voyage to Atlantis   James W. Mavor

The Renaissance   Walter Pater

Temple of the Stars
Brinsley le Poer Trench

The Letters of Vincent Van Gogh
Edited by Mark Roskill

Renaissance and Baroque
Heinrich Wölfflin